Peter de Figueiredo | Julian Treuherz

111 Places in Manchester That You Shouldn't Miss

emons:

© Bibliographical information of the Deutsche Nationalbibliothek
The Deutsche Nationalbibliothek lists this publication in
the Deutsche Nationalbibliografie; detailed bibliographical data
are available on the internet at http://dnb.d-nb.de.

© Emons Verlag GmbH
Cäcilienstraße 48, 50667 Köln
info@emons-verlag.de
All rights reserved
© Photographs by Peter de Figueiredo, except:
Banners of the People (ch. 11) © People's History Museum
Egyptian tomb (ch. 33) © Bolton Council
John Rylands Library Entrance (ch. 55) © University of Manchester
Manchester City Changing Room (ch. 66) © Manchester City FC
Valette's *Albert Square* (ch. 104) © Manchester Art Gallery/Bridgeman Images
© Cover image: shutterstock.com/Shahril KHMD
Layout: Conny Laue, based on a design by Lübbeke | Naumann | Thoben
Maps: altancicek.design, www.altancicek.de
Basic cartographical information from Openstreetmap,
© OpenStreetMap-Mitwirkende, OdbL
Editing: Ros Horton
Printing and binding: sourc-e GmbH
Printed in Europe 2025
ISBN 978-3-7408-2645-1
Revised fifth edition, June 2025

Guidebooks for Locals & Experienced Travellers
Join us in uncovering new places around the world at
www.111places.com

Foreword

Manchester was made by the Industrial Revolution: from the late 18th century until World War I it grew rapidly, changing from market town to industrial city, and from manufacturing centre to commercial hub. It pioneered new forms of transport based on canals and railways; it created the Ship Canal, which made it an international port, and built Trafford Park, the first planned industrial estate in the world. In politics, Manchester led the country, promoting free trade and women's suffrage. The 20th century brought economic decline and loss of prestige, symbolised by the *Manchester Guardian* dropping the name of the city from its masthead in 1959 and moving to London shortly after. However, the city fought back, its renaissance led by a strong financial services sector and cultural innovation – Coronation Street, the Royal Exchange Theatre and Madchester, the innovative music scene of the 1980s.

Manchester today is again in transition. Swathes of post-industrial dereliction have been redeveloped and rebranded – Media City, Ancoats, Castlefield, Spinningfields, and the Northern Quarter. The worst mistakes of the 1960s, such as the Hulme Crescents, have been expunged, and although the ugly Arndale Centre survived the 1996 IRA bomb, the attack speeded up a process of urban regeneration already begun some years earlier.

The City of Manchester is relatively small, but it is the hub of a large conurbation, the Greater Manchester city-region, encompassing Salford as well as former factory towns such as Rochdale, Oldham, Bolton and Stockport. These satellite towns are now beginning to follow Manchester's example and reinvent themselves with cultural and leisure attractions catering for increasingly sophisticated urban pleasure-seekers. The harsh, gritty quality inherited from the region's industrial past is part of their appeal. This is our personal selection of the region's offbeat delights and we hope you enjoy them.

111 Places

1__ 20 Stories
Way up there | 10

2__ 31 Toad Lane
Birthplace of the Co-op | 12

3__ Afflecks
A visit to retroland | 14

4__ Alexandra Park, Oldham
Oldham's green oasis | 16

5__ Altrincham Market
Food, flowers, fads and fashion | 18

6__ Ancoats Mills
No longer dark and satanic | 20

7__ Angel Meadow
Park with a hidden past | 22

8__ Anita Street
A street for crossword addicts? | 24

9__ Another Hand
All hands on deck | 26

10__ Anthony Burgess Foundation
Haunt of the literati | 28

11__ Banners of the People
From Whit Walks to Ban the Bomb | 30

12__ Barton Arcade
Under crystal domes | 32

13__ Barton Swing Aqueduct
A wonder of the waterway world | 34

14__ Beaumont Organic
The future of fashion? | 36

15__ Blackfriars
Two nations: the rich and the poor | 38

16__ The Boulder in the Quad
When the Lake District came to Manchester | 40

17__ Bridgewater Basin
Aquatic urban oasis | 42

18__ Britannia Hotel (formerly Watts Warehouse)
Domain of a merchant prince | 44

19 — Bury Market
Black pudding and Chorley cakes | 46

20 — Castlefield Railway Viaducts
The march of the giants | 48

21 — Cathedral Choir
'Rabbit's Revenge' | 50

22 — Central Ref
Therefore get wisdom | 52

23 — Chinese Garden at RHS Bridgewater
Painting a picture in plants | 54

24 — Chorlton Water Park
Grebes, bats and hula hoops | 56

25 — Closing Cotton Prices at the Royal Exchange
The end of an era | 58

26 — Contact Theatre
The face of carbon zero | 60

27 — The Curry Mile
India on a plate | 62

28 — Dale Street
Filming the Big Apple | 64

29 — Deadstock General Store
Retail is detail | 66

30 — Dormouse Chocolates
Manchester's first bean to bar | 68

31 — East Lancashire Railway
Steaming ahead | 70

32 — Edgar Wood in Middleton
Artistry in architecture | 72

33 — Egyptian Tomb
Journey into the netherworld | 74

34 — Elizabeth Gaskell's House
Victorian literary life | 76

35 — Ellenroad Engine House
The world's biggest working steam engine | 78

36 — Engels' Beard
Radical facial hair | 80

37 — esea contemporary
Small gallery, global reach | 82

38 — FAC 251
Where Factory Records ended its days | 84

39 __ Fairfield Moravian Settlement
Village of vision | 86

40 __ Fireground
Fighting the flames | 88

41 __ Form Lifestyle Store
Small but perfectly formed | 90

42 __ Frank Sidebottom
The man with the papier-mâché head | 92

43 __ Free Trade Hall
Where the Madchester sound took root | 94

44 __ Gay Village
A proud history of queer culture | 96

45 __ George Best's Mini
Booze, birds and fast cars | 98

46 __ The Glade of Light
Memorial to the Arena Bombing | 100

47 __ Hallé St Peter's
Bringing music to the people | 102

48 __ Hanging Ditch
An ancient bridge revealed | 104

49 __ Hat Works
Historical headgear | 106

50 __ Haweswater Aqueduct Mural
A neglected Manchester sculptor | 108

51 __ Higher Ground
Casual dining, seasonal sharing | 110

52 __ Holy Name of Jesus
Masterpiece by the designer of the hansom cab | 112

53 __ Imperial War Museum North
Deconstructivism at Salford Quays | 114

54 __ Jandol
Lebanese delight | 116

55 __ John Rylands Library Entrance Hall
Valhalla of the book | 118

56 __ Karl Marx's Desk
The oldest public library in Britain | 120

57 __ Kiku
Glamour in the Northern Quarter | 122

58 __ Kim's Kitchen
Brutalism meets kitsch | 124

59 — Kimpton Clock Tower Hotel
Tiles by the mile | 126

60 — LANX
Choose Lancashire shoes | 128

61 — Lark Hill Place
Remembrance of Salford past | 130

62 — Legh Road, Knutsford
The Witches' Sabbath | 132

63 — Library Walk Link
A beautiful folly? | 134

64 — Little David Street
A secret place revealed | 136

65 — Mackie Mayor
Cuisine from eight kitchens | 138

66 — Man City Changing Room
The Soul of the Squad | 140

67 — The Manchester Baby
Freddie's world-changing computer | 142

68 — Manchester Jewish Museum
Look, listen, learn and eat | 144

69 — Manchester Poplars
As seen in St John's Gardens | 146

70 — Marble Arch
Pub with a theatrical touch | 148

71 — Mark Addy Memorial
The people's hero | 150

72 — Mayfield Park
From Grot Spot to Green Space | 152

73 — Minut Men
Concrete totems of the sixties | 154

74 — The Monastery
Lifting the spirits | 156

75 — the modernist
Celebrating brutalism | 158

76 — Monument to Vimto
Have you got the bottle? | 160

77 — Mr Lowry's Stockport
Dominated by the viaduct | 162

78 — Mr Thomas's Chop House
Manchester's first gastropub | 164

79___ National Cycling Centre
Sport, speed and centrifugal force | 166

80___ Ordsall Hall
Old house, new garden | 168

81___ The Pankhurst Centre
Where the suffragette movement began | 170

82___ Peterloo Memorial
Manchester's massacre of the innocents | 172

83___ Peveril of the Peak
Here's to Nancy | 174

84___ Plaza Cinema
Stockport's silver screen | 176

85___ Police Museum
A night in the slammer | 178

86___ Portico Library
Hidden literary oasis | 180

87___ Post Box, Corporation Street
It survived the IRA bomb | 182

88___ Private White V.C.
British craftsmanship at its best | 184

89___ Richmond Tea Rooms
Through the looking glass | 186

90___ Rochdale Town Hall
Municipal magnificence | 188

91___ Runaway Brewery
Behind the scenes at the microbrewery | 190

92___ Salford Lads' Club
Not just for Smiths fans | 192

93___ Sifters
When Liam and Noel were still speaking | 194

94___ Southern Cemetery Gates
The gates that inspired Morrissey | 196

95___ The Spärrows
Cross-border comfort food | 198

96___ Sperm Whale Skeleton
300 dollars' worth of bones | 200

97___ St George's, Stockport
And glory shone around | 202

98___ Staircase House
A historic house you can touch | 204

99 — Stockport Air Raid Shelters
The Chestergate Hotel | 206

100 — The Temple
From water closet to watering place | 208

101 — Tower of Light
The world's most beautiful flue | 210

102 — Twenty Twenty Two
Bats in the basement | 212

103 — Unicorn Grocery
Did you bring your own bag? | 214

104 — Valette's Albert Square
Still in the heart of Manchester | 216

105 — Victoria Baths
A water palace refreshed | 218

106 — Walkden Gardens
A garden of many rooms | 220

107 — The Wash House
Rinse and spin | 222

108 — Where the Light Gets In
Not so much a meal as an experience | 224

109 — Whitworth Garden
Art in the park | 226

110 — Worsley Delph
Coals to Manchester | 228

111 — Yes
Positive thinking on four floors | 230

1 20 Stories
Way up there

An outdoor rooftop bar in Manchester might seem a bit chancy, but try getting into 20 Stories on a Saturday night and you will have to join a queue of twenty-somethings dressed to the nines – no tracksuits, flip-flops or football shirts, but tailored shorts are allowed up to 7pm. It is worth the wait – or you can go early. Take the lift to the 19th storey (there isn't a 20th); in case you are wondering why it's called 20 Stories, the punning name is a woolly PR concept about the tales of Mancunian history, culture and music enshrined in the menu. The food in the restaurant is heavenly and much of it is locally sourced, but the prices go through the roof (the real explanation for the name?). Forget about dinner unless you are on a footballer's salary and go for the better-value weekend brunch. But the really great things here are the terrace bar, the cocktails and the view.

At the terrace bar there is a fabulous drinks menu with classic cocktails for the suits and signature creations such as Manchester Tart Punch (with fresh raspberries and cream) for the high heels and leopard print tights. For those worried about the weather, the terrace has tall glass screens to keep off the wind, and you can shelter from the drizzle in see-through igloos decorated with plastic flowers (the trees are real). If the rain is really bad you can always take refuge in the indoor bar with its stylish black-and-white supersofas, but this would be a pity because the view is phenomenal.

Some people might find the Manchester townscape boringly flat, but here it comes into its own with a 360° panorama going as far as the Pennines on one side and Cheshire on the other; down below are the city's domes, rooftops and cranes. Don't forget to go to the loo, as the bits you can't see from the terrace are visible from the floor-to-ceiling corridor windows. If it's all a bit vertigo-inducing, just go easy on the cocktails.

Address No. 1 Spinningfields, 1 Hardman Square, Manchester M3 3EB, +44 (0)161 204 3333, www.20stories.co.uk | Getting there 8-minute walk from St. Peter's Square | Hours Mon–Wed noon–11pm, Thu noon–midnight, Fri & Sat noon–1am, Sun noon–11pm | Tip At 14 storeys, Sunlight House, near the corner of Deansgate and Quay Street, was Manchester's first skyscraper, built in 1932 by Russian emigré architect Joseph Sunlight. The swimming pool in the basement, now part of a health club, was opened by film star Douglas Fairbanks.

2 31 Toad Lane
Birthplace of the Co-op

The first Co-op shop in the world opened on 21 December, 1844 in this modest Georgian warehouse in Rochdale. Initially it sold only butter, sugar, flour and oatmeal, a far cry from today's Co-op supermarkets, banks and insurance companies. The shop was started by the Rochdale Pioneers, a society based on co-operation, fairness, self-help, equality and democracy. Anyone could join; members had an equal share in decision-making and an equal share in the profits (the famous divi). The Pioneers was the first successful Co-operative Society, the model for similar organisations that sprang up across Britain and all over the world. Co-ops are particularly widespread in Japan: at Kobe there is even a full-size replica of 31 Toad Lane.

The Rochdale building was refurbished in 2012. Inside is a delightful small museum with an evocative reconstruction of the original shop: stone-flagged floor, simple wooden counter, sacks of oatmeal and flour, a cone of sugar and a large lump of butter (a rather obvious replica). In the display area you can see the first Minute Book of the society (first resolution: to buy a Minute Book), a velvet cap worn by Robert Owen, the 'Father of Co-operation', Co-op biscuit tins, bicycles and examples of packaging and advertising featuring the Wheatsheaf, which was used as a symbol of co-operation – one ear of wheat does not stand up on its own but bound together with others it is strong. Upstairs is a projection area where you can watch old promotional films including Co-operette, a hilarious 1930s musical comedy featuring dancing vegetables. In the fast-moving business environment of today, the Co-operative movement faces many challenges but its founding principles are still relevant, and it has embraced new causes such as sustainability and climate change. It is a humbling thought that it all began in the small industrial town of Rochdale.

Address 31 Toad Lane, Rochdale OL12 0NU, +44 (0)1706 524920, www.rochdalepioneersmuseum.coop | **Getting there** Tram to Rochdale Town Centre (pink line) and 5-minute walk | **Hours** Wed–every other Sat 10.30am–4pm (check website before visiting) | **Tip** Opposite, in front of the church of St Mary in the Baum, is a memorial stone to those who died in the Kobe earthquake of 1995. The stone was laid in the presence of co-operators from Japan, Sweden, Germany and Great Britain.

3 Afflecks
A visit to retroland

Once upon a time, Affleck & Brown was an elegant department store in Oldham Street where ladies shopped for gowns, furs and dressmaking materials. In the 1960s, Oldham Street went downhill as Manchester shopping became concentrated around Market Street, St Ann's Square and Deansgate, and the store closed in 1973. In 1982 it reopened as Affleck's Palace, an alternative shopping venue, and despite two fires and a change of management in 2008, when the name was shortened to Afflecks, it has continued as an emporium for everything that is not mainstream in fashion, style and adornment. Over 60 independent small businesses are jumbled together in a labyrinth of stalls on four floors.

For the intrepid explorer wanting to make sense of teenage culture, an expedition to Afflecks is essential. It's the ideal place to study the latest trends in tattoos or sunglasses; you can have your nose pierced or your hair done (all styles catered for including the way-out); buy tarot cards, runes and crystals; add to your collection of games; acquire a Star Wars droid or a Zippo cigarette lighter; or try out UV make-up with cruelty free glitter. By now the urban anthropologist may find their head swimming from too much exposure to psychedelic poster designs or Pokemon cards, and require some refreshments. It's time for a fry up or a toastie at Third Floor Rising or (even better) an ice cream at Ginger's Comfort Emporium, before resuming the tour.

By far the largest category of merchandise at Afflecks is clothing – there is plenty of street fashion in the form of T-shirts, hoodies and jeans, but even more pervasive are the stalls selling old clothes. Here, hidden codes are at work that have elevated second-hand into the more stylish 'vintage' category – not to be confused with 'retro', meaning new but looks old. Only one thing is certain – the kids will grow out of it just like we did.

Address 52 Church Street, Manchester M4 1PW, +44 (0)161 839 0718, www.afflecks.com | **Getting there** Tram (most lines) or bus to Piccadilly Gardens | **Hours** Mon–Fri 10.30am–6pm, Sat 10am–6pm, Sun 11am–5pm | **Tip** Catch a gig at the Band on the Wall, Manchester's celebrated music venue at 25–27 Swan Street, which hosts sessions by top names in jazz, folk, rap and world music.

4 Alexandra Park, Oldham
Oldham's green oasis

When Oldham was badly hit by the Lancashire Cotton Famine as a result of the American Civil War, a proposal to build a public park in 1863 was only approved on condition that unemployed cotton workers be engaged to construct it. The relief effort duly provided the town with one of the best-loved parks in the north of England. The designer was William Henderson whose layout cleverly combines formality with the picturesque. It is based around a formal terrace from which the land falls away to the south giving views over the town's surviving cotton mills. At each end of the terrace are statues of local worthies: James Platt, a leading textile manufacturer, supported by four bronze female figures representing Engineering, Mathematics, Art and Science; and Robert Ashworth, who is inscribed *The Workers' Friend*. At the mid-point is a decorative shelter known as The Lion's Den, from which a cross walk runs down the centre of the park with a pool and fountain on the axis. Paths lead off to less formal areas including a large boating lake and a smaller lake, both teeming with wildlife. To the south-west is a well-stocked conservatory with domed lantern and a quirky Chinese pagoda-style observatory. Alongside this is a statue of 'Old Blind Joe', Oldham's official bellman from 1820 to 1860, paid for by public subscription. Nearby are two large geological specimens, and another path leads across a bridge over the former 'Lovers' Walk'.

The park opened in 1865, and although some of the buildings and statues were added later, it remains largely unchanged from its original design and is beautifully maintained. On summer evenings you will see families strolling, picnicking and admiring the landscape in just the way it was intended. Oldham suffered decline and shoddy redevelopment in the later 20th century, but Alexandra Park still shows how it was in its industrial heyday.

Address Kings Road, Oldham OL8 2BN, +44 (0)161 770 4056, www.oldham.gov.uk | Getting there Tram to Oldham Mumps (pink line) and bus 425 to Glodwick Road | Hours Daily dawn–dusk | Tip Oldham Town Hall, a handsome Greek Revival building, abandoned by the council in the 1980s and declared Britain's most endangered historic structure, has recently been well restored and converted to a cinema.

5 — Altrincham Market
Food, flowers, fads and fashion

Curated is the word that springs to mind when visiting Altrincham Covered Market – it has a remarkable group of traders, each with something special to offer. Exceptional sourdough bread is made by Aidan Monks at Lovingly Artisan: his Malted Barley won the Bread of the Year award, and there are plenty of other unusual loaves such as Spiced Apple, or Cheddar and Chilli. The Market Fresh Flowers stall is an appealing sight with its subtly coloured seasonal flowers and leaves, combined to make customised rustic bouquets. You can also buy organic, locally-grown fruit and vegetables, tempting cheeses, home-made cakes and the freshest fish, but even more of a treat than the produce stalls are the traders selling goods that you won't easily find anywhere else. One Small Step is Rachael Wong's zero-waste stall with refillable cleaning products, plastic-free toiletries, reusable beeswax food wraps and biodegradable bamboo toothbrushes as well as unpackaged pastas, seeds and grains to take away in your own containers. A jollier note is struck by Swank, where you can buy Susan Baxter's colourful vintage-style headwraps, sunglasses, crazily patterned socks and scarves. Joe & Co. is a hard-to-find Lancashire brand selling limited edition jeans and workwear in raw selvedge denim and linen and wool grandad shirts which will appeal to the stylish male; while for the stylish dog, B&V Trading has a colourful display of dog-collars, leads, coats and harnesses in stripes, checks, tartan and paisley, as well as bowls, whistles and doggy treats. There is a stall for Fire Station Square Pottery, made in Salford, and another for The Sculpts, a range of tiles, prints and badges with clever alphabetical designs inspired by Manchester's architecture and heritage.

Next to the Market is the Market House, precursor of Mackie Mayor in Manchester (see ch. 65) – the success of all three is a tribute to the 'passionately regional philosophy' of their founder Nick Johnson.

Address Greenwood Street, Altrincham WA14 1SA, www.altrinchammarket.website | **Getting there** Train or tram (Altrincham line) to Altrincham and 5-minute walk | **Hours** Tue & Fri 8am–3pm, Sat 8am–4pm, Sun 10am–4pm; Antiques and bric-à-brac: Thu 8am–4pm; Producers/crafts: first Fri every month 8am–2pm | **Tip** Altrincham town centre was developed by the Earls of Stamford. You can visit their country house, Dunham Massey (National Trust) – 15-minute bus ride on CAT5 bus from Altrincham Interchange.

6 Ancoats Mills
No longer dark and satanic

In 1826, the great German neoclassical architect Karl Friedrich Schinkel visited Manchester and made a sketch of McConnel and Kennedy's Mill in Redhill Street, Ancoats. 'One sees buildings where, three years ago, there were only meadows, but the buildings are so black that they look as if they have been used for one hundred years,' he wrote. This enormous steam-powered works, eight storeys high, also shocked the Frenchman Alexis de Tocqueville in 1835 when he discovered that it housed 1,500 workers labouring 69 hours a week, three-quarters of whom were women or children. James McConnel and John Kennedy, two self-made Scotsmen, had built their cotton spinning mill fronting the Rochdale Canal in 1818. Now known as Sedgwick Mill, it was altered by William Fairbairn in 1865 to accommodate more modern machinery, and then expanded over the next 50 years both at the rear and on the western side where the Royal Mill was added. This vast complex, together with the equally large Murrays' Mills that adjoin it on the eastern side, form a sheer cliff of brickwork overlooking the canal, and have long symbolised the brutality of the Industrial Revolution.

Yet they have survived, and after years of decline have taken on new life as work-places and apartments. You can explore the Royal and Sedgwick Mills by entering the impressive glazed atrium that encloses the former courtyard. Here you will find Ancoats Coffee, with a great selection of specialist coffees and tasty sandwiches, and on display is a large-scale model of the mill complex that explains its history. Though the mills no longer roar with the perpetual whirl and clatter of machinery, on winter evenings you might still imagine the sight that so impressed the hero of Disraeli's novel *Coningsby* of 'illuminated factories with more windows than Italian palaces and smoking chimneys taller than Egyptian obelisks.'

Address Redhill Street, Ancoats, M33 3EL | Getting there Bus 76, 83, 181 182 to Oldham Road/ New Cross and 5-minutes walk | Hours Ancoats Coffee Mon–Fri 8.30am–5pm, Sat 9am–5pm, Sun 10am–5pm | Tip In nearby New Islington, by the Ashton Canal, is Chips, an apartment block designed by Will Alsop for Urban Splash offering a contemporary take on the Ancoats Mills.

7 Angel Meadow
Park with a hidden past

This moderately sized area of grass and trees divided by a low brick wall, looks nothing special, but it is redolent with history. The land between the River Irk and Rochdale Road was first developed in the late 18th century as a genteel semi-rural suburb of Georgian houses. The church of St Michael and All Angels opened in 1789 (the wall ran along the edge of the churchyard) but soon the banks of the river attracted mills, foundries, dyeworks and timber yards. The wealthy began to move out as a large influx of people arrived seeking factory work, lodging in cheaply built housing. Gasworks, the railway, more factories and the stench of the polluted river sealed Angel Meadow's fate. It turned into an overcrowded and insanitary slum.

One of its most notorious features was the pauper's burial ground, built on the level plot beyond the churchyard wall, where an estimated 40,000 people were buried: Engels described the putrefying bodies filling the neighbourhood with 'revolting and injurious gases.' The cemetery had to be closed and covered in stone flags although it has since been grassed over: the human remains found there have been reburied at Southern Cemetery.

L. S. Lowry, whose grandparents lived nearby on Oldham Road, made several paintings of the church, which was demolished in 1935 and the area suffered badly in the Blitz. Post-war it continued to be a pocket of deprivation, with lodging houses and charity schools (Ancoats-born Violet Carson, *Coronation Street*'s Ena Sharples, was a supporter of the Sharp Street Ragged Schools in the 1970s).

By the millennium, Angel Meadow was all but forgotten, but today blocks of luxury apartments loom up above it, a textbook example of urban cycles of rise, decline and regeneration. Full marks to the Friends of Angel Meadow for initiating the restoration of the park and bringing its forgotten history to life.

Address Angel Street, Manchester M4 4BR | **Getting there** Tram (most lines) or train to Victoria and 10-minute walk | **Hours** Daily dawn–dusk | **Tip** In Arch 5 of the nearby viaduct facing Corporation Street is Popup Bikes, which sells second-hand bikes, parts and cycling books, does same-day bike repairs and serves coffee and cakes. Motto: 'We love coffee, we love bikes, we love cyclists.'

8 Anita Street
A street for crossword addicts?

Tucked away in Ancoats is a small group of municipal houses built in 1897, with the latest mod cons of the time: running cold water and pull-the-chain flush toilets. This was a model of clean living in a densely packed area of miserable slum housing, thunderous engineering factories and huge mills all belching out black smoke.

Ancoats has been called the world's first industrial suburb, its rapid growth in the early 19th century driven by canal building and steam-powered manufacturing, and clustered inside this frenetic hive of industry were overcrowded dwellings built for the workers, often of the meanest and most insanitary kind. Replacement of the worst housing commenced in the 1890s when the Corporation formed an 'Unhealthy Dwellings Committee', and one of their main priorities was Ancoats. Here, a mass of back-to-back slum houses was pulled down and replaced by the first municipal housing in the city, a huge courtyard block of flats and three rows of two-storey houses, including Anita Street, all of which survive today. The accommodation was quite basic, but most Ancoats labourers could not afford the rents, and families had to uproot themselves from the area to find cheaper and less healthy dwellings elsewhere.

The courtyard block, Victoria Square, is five storeys high, with corner turrets originally containing laundries and drying rooms and continuous access balconies within the courtyard. Centred on it is Anita Street, its modest terraced homes well restored and neatly painted, with the roadway now closed to traffic so that the inhabitants can sit outside in the sunshine.

Originally it was called Sanitary Street after the Manchester and Salford Sanitary Association, but the residents objected to the 's' word. In an attempt to remove the stigma and give the street a more refined aura, the 's' and the 'ry' were dropped. So Anita never existed!

Address Anita Street, Manchester M4 5DU | **Getting there** Bus 76, 83, 181 182 to Oldham Road/New Cross | **Tip** Another survival of pioneer social reform in Ancoats is the former Methodist Women's Night Shelter on the corner of George Leigh Street and Great Ancoats Street. Built in 1893, it gave help to homeless women.

9 Another Hand
All hands on deck

The creation of two chefs, Julian Pizer of late-lamented 3hands deli and Max Yorke, formerly with Hispi, and baker Danny Foggo of Holy Grain, Another Hand is not just another fancy restaurant. In fact, it's not fancy at all – with exposed brick and blockwork and an industrial feel it was largely built by the team themselves. The kitchen is on open display, and a large counter on which the food is meticulously prepared is the focus of attention. Simple wooden tables, Ercol-type chairs and orange upholstered banquettes, along with pictures and houseplants are the only furnishings. The back of the kitchen is clad in shiny dark green tiles. But it's the superbly well-balanced food here that really counts.

The format is sharing plates, based on responsibly farmed seasonal produce. You might start with a grilled chicken skewer its flavour complemented by leek, wild mushroom and caramelised filo; or halloumi soaked in fermented honey, the cheese sourced from Martin Gott's St. James Farm, Cumbria. The humble carrot reaches new heights of deliciousness when braised and served with smoked ketchup, carrot top pesto, pine nut and gooseberry; ditto the beetroot, smoked and accompanied by charcoal cream, ruby grapefruit and horseradish. Meat offerings might include fallow deer, salt-glazed duck or glazed lamb rump with anchovy sauce vierge. A whole roasted sea bream comes with brown butter, yuzu, kombu and smoked chilli. For the sweet of tooth there is Basque burnt cheesecake with pears, or warm rye chocolate with blood orange and spiced gingerbread. The wine list includes many natural and organic wines, carefully chosen to suit the food and the enthusiastic staff are happy to advise.

Don't be put off by the unusual combinations. 'The dishes are so inventive in terms of flavour and texture, but without pretension' explains a satisfied customer. That's what makes Another Hand so special.

Address Unit F 253 Deansgate, Mews Level, Manchester M3 4EN, +44 (0)161 834 2988, https://anotherhandmcr.com | **Getting there** Tram to Deansgate-Castlefield (all lines) | **Hours** Wed–Sat noon–2pm & 5–11pm | **Tip** If you tasted the bread at Another Hand you'll want a sourdough loaf from the Holy Grain next door but one to take home.

10 Anthony Burgess Foundation
Haunt of the literati

The sign outside says Burgess but people think it's burgers. Anthony Burgess was born in Manchester in 1917. From humble beginnings in Harpurhey, miles Platting and Moss Side, where his parents ran a pub, he rose to become a literary giant, writing 33 novels, 25 non-fiction titles, 2 volumes of autobiography, 3 symphonies, over 250 other musical works and thousands of essays, reviews, newspaper articles and film scripts. Burgess studied English Literature at Manchester University, and became a schoolteacher before his career as a writer took off. His novels are satires on modern society, witty, often bizarre, and pessimistic about the future.

In his later years he lived a rootless existence, an outsider moving between England, Italy and France, ending up as a tax exile in Monaco, but Manchester never left him – although you would never know it from his accent. He rejected religion but the Bible stories learned at his Catholic schools in Manchester run through many of his books. His most famous novel, *A Clockwork Orange*, which became better known through Stanley Kubrick's film, is a dystopian fantasy exploring violent teenage subculture: the book is written in an invented language that mixes the criminal argot first encountered by Burgess in Manchester gang culture with the slang of the Russian and American underworlds.

After his death in 1993, his widow donated many of his papers to the University of Texas, but in 2003 she established the International Anthony Burgess Foundation in Manchester, where the larger part of his archive is housed in a 19th-century building that was once a mackintosh factory. The Foundation hosts special events such as concerts, talks and debates. It is fronted by the Burgess Bar, open only during events, a muzak-free zone where you can buy Burgess books, posters and CDs as well as drinks – but no burgers.

Address Engine House, Chorlton Mill, 3 Cambridge Street, Manchester M1 5BY, +44 (0)161 235 0776, www.anthonyburgess.org | **Getting there** Train to Oxford Road, or tram to St Peter's Square (all lines) and 10-minute walk | **Hours** The Foundation can be visited for archive research by appointment. For special events see website. | **Tip** Two blocks away on Great Marlborough Street a plaque records the site of Little Ireland, an early 19th-century area of slum housing where Irish workers lived in overcrowded conditions of indescribable filth.

11 Banners of the People
From Whit Walks to Ban the Bomb

'Carshalton Left Book Club. The Pen is mightier than the Sword.' 'Votes for Women. Believe and you will Conquer.' 'Ipswich Dockers Union. Unity is Strength.' 'Kensington Young Communists say Jobs not Bombs.' 'Lesbians and Gay Men Out and Proud.' 'Hyde Socialist Sunday School. Virtue for our Armour, Justice for our Sword.' 'People's March for Jobs.' These are just a few of the slogans painted, embroidered, appliquéd and printed on banners in the collection of the People's History Museum. Some are crudely made from cheap materials, others lovingly crafted by professional banner artists – all of them with vivid stories to tell of working-class culture, protest, affirmation of ideals and rights fought for, won or denied.

The museum, in a former hydraulic pumping station, has a particular angle on British history – not kings and queens, generals and treaties, but working men and women, their daily lives and their struggles for democratic representation over the last 200 years. Their stories are told through the aura of objects – a truncheon used at a Chartist meeting, the table at which Thomas Paine wrote *The Rights of Man*, Michael Foot's donkey jacket and Harold Wilson's pipe – and through many significant collections – 2,000 election posters, 300 political cartoons and 7,000 trades union badges and tokens.

Unique to this museum is the collection of 400 banners, the largest and most important such collection in the world, bringing immediacy and impact to the displays. Banner conservation is also a specialism but most of them cannot be kept on permanent display because of their fragility. All but a few are changed annually, and one of the pleasures of visiting the museum is to see which new banners the curators come up with each year after the January changeover. When you have seen the displays, check out the shop – some of the banners make great tea towels.

Address Left Bank, Spinningfields, Manchester M3 3ER, +44 (0)161 838 9190, www.phm.org.uk | **Getting there** Free bus (route 1) to Bridge Street, or train to Salford Central and 5-minute walk | **Hours** Wed–Mon 10am–5pm | **Tip** More working-class history in nearby Wood Street (reached via Bradley's Court): the 1905 Working Men's Church, linked to the Wood Street Mission, is a Victorian charity that still helps poor families with food and clothing.

12 Barton Arcade
Under crystal domes

When passing the ponderous stone façade at 51–63 Deansgate you would never know that behind it is one of the most beautiful Victorian shopping arcades in Britain. Walk inside and the spirits are immediately lifted even on the greyest of Manchester days, when the light floods in through the glass vaults and domes that soar overhead. Tiers of slender ironwork balconies with scrolly supports make delicate patterns against the sky and draw the eye around the curving lines of the galleries.

The roof may have been influenced by the Galleria Vittorio Emanuele II in Milan that dates from 1867, but the iron structure of the Manchester building was assembled on site in 1871 from components manufactured by Macfarlane's Saracen foundry in Glasgow. The Saracen works was one of greatest manufacturers of architectural ironwork, and their products were shipped around the Empire, but a combination of wartime bombing of the foundry and the government's order to recover iron artefacts to increase armaments production sadly destroyed much of the company's contribution to the world.

The arcade has had its ups and downs. In the 1980s it was largely empty and seriously decayed, but since then it has been restored and has attracted some eye-catching stores and restaurants. These include Jeffery-West, purveyors of shoes and boots for men of fashion and Barber Barber for your clipper cut and beard sculpt. The R Store has all the latest brands in mens Heritage style streetwear, sportswear and Americana, but advises its customers that it is 'A shop which only stocks stuff that we like. If you do not appreciate this idea please go directly to the Arndale Centre.' Have a relaxing coffee and croissant or classic breakfast with an Aussie accent at Pot Kettle Black where you can sit out in the arcade and admire the glass domes floating high above.

Address 51–63 Deansgate/48 Barton Square, Manchester M3 2BH, +44 (0)161 219 3535, www.barton-arcade.co.uk | Getting there Free bus (route 2) to Royal Exchange | Tip In the centre of nearby St Ann's Square is an intriguing fountain by Peter Randall-Page of a pink granite cotton boll on a dark stone base.

13 Barton Swing Aqueduct
A wonder of the waterway world

The swing aqueduct that carries the Bridgewater Canal over the Manchester Ship Canal was an unprecedented work of engineering when it opened in 1893. It replaced the earlier Barton Aqueduct, a masonry structure of 1761 by Richard Brindley that took the Bridgewater Canal over the River Irwell, but since vessels using the mighty ship canal were much larger than the old river boats, the new aqueduct had to be movable. The daring solution devised by Sir Edward Leader Williams, engineer for the ship canal, was to rotate the iron water trough weighing 1,450 tonnes on a pivot mounted on a narrow, purpose-built island in the centre of the ship canal. In order to retain the water within the trough, iron gates drop down at each end, with additional gates on each bank retaining the water in the respective stretches of canal.

At the same time, Williams built a swing road bridge alongside, both structures being operated from a brick control tower at the central point on the island. When in the open position, the aqueduct and road bridge line up along the length of the island, allowing ships to traverse on each side. To avoid any risk of collision, the aqueduct is opened half an hour before the vessel on the ship canal is scheduled to pass.

The original turning mechanism survives and is built into the central island. It consists of upper and lower race plates, the lower ones embedded in granite blocks and separated from the upper ones by roller bearings. The mechanism was originally powered by a hydraulic engine supplied with steam from two Lancashire boilers housed in a pumping station on the Eccles bank of the ship canal, but in 1939 the hydraulic engines were replaced by a pair of three-cylinder engines. It is a thrilling sight to witness what is the world's first and only swing aqueduct on the move, with the massive ship canal stretched out below.

Address Chapel Place, Urmston M41 7LE | **Getting there** Train to Patricroft and 15-minute walk | **Tip** All Saints Roman Catholic church is the masterpiece of E. W. Pugin and was built in 1868. The church is now owned by the Greyfriars monks and is not currently open to visit, but it can be clearly viewed from Redclyffe Road alongside the ship canal.

14_ Beaumont Organic
The future of fashion?

The little shopfront in the Georgian brick terrace is painted a traditional green. Inside, all is light and airy with white walls, pale wood flooring and cream upholstery. What makes this womenswear shop special is that everything is ethically sourced and made from sustainable natural fabrics with fully traceable footprints: all aspects of supply and manufacture have been considered in order to cut down on unnecessary waste and minimise damage to the environment.

Fabrics include organic cotton from certified farms in Europe, traditionally produced Italian linen, plant-based materials such as bamboo and lyocell (manufactured from wood pulp) and lambswool from free-roaming Scottish sheep. The clothing is made in trusted factories mainly in Portugal or Britain, transported by road and packed in cardboard boxes. Waste is avoided by ordering only as much fabric as is needed, and leather goods are made from offcuts.

The distinctive brand was launched by Mancunian Hannah Beaumont-Laurencia in 2008 with just eight organic cotton T-shirts, and now sells a wide range of original designs online and at retailers all over the world. Hannah opened the Manchester shop in 2017, with the design studio and company office on the first floor. The shop is the only place where you can see her entire collection, including homewares such as baskets and candles. The clothes show that ethical need not mean spartan or frumpy: textures are luxuriously soft, and the styling has the kind of simplicity that comes from sophisticated cutting, combining loose silhouettes with elegant line. There are no frills or lurid colours, and no artificial dyes. Although two seasonal collections are produced each year, the garments are classic in style, designed to be worn again and again – the antithesis of instant throwaway fashion. Beaumont was ahead of the curve in 2008: will the fashion world ever catch up?

Address 49 Hilton Street, Manchester M1 2EF, +44 (0)161 971 9010, www.beaumontorganic.com | **Getting there** 5 minute-walk from Piccadilly Gardens | **Hours** Wed–Fri 11am–6pm, Sat 10am–5pm | **Tip** Nearby, at 1A Stevenson Square is Unitom, a specialist bookshop with an astonishing collection of visual art orientated books, magazines, prints and editions.

15 Blackfriars
Two nations: the rich and the poor

Look over the parapet of the Blackfriars Bridge crossing the Irwell and you will see the river banks lined with tall apartment blocks and smart hotels, linked by a riverside walkway. In Victorian times Blackfriars was one of the most deprived parts of the city. The Frenchman Alexis de Tocqueville visited the area in 1835 and described the marshy land at river level with its muddy ditches and meagre one-storey houses as 'the final refuge for a man torn between poverty and death.' His famous statement 'From this foul drain the greatest stream of human industry flows out to fertilise the whole world. From this filthy sewer pure gold flows…' compares the appalling conditions of the workers with the vast riches made by the manufacturing class. Wages were kept low by the presence of large numbers of Irish immigrants, labour relations were bad and disease among the poorest was rife.

Unlike today, the riverside was hidden away, never visited by the middle or upper classes. The huge gulf between rich and poor was an accepted fact, and most novelists and journalists would write from a moralistic viewpoint about escape from poverty to riches, rather than the reality of life in the slums. Yet there were official reports describing serious overcrowding and insanitary conditions: a cellar dwelling housing 18 people, 2 or 3 to a bed; a narrow passage off Deansgate with one privy serving 380 inhabitants; and countless descriptions of dampness, overflowing privies and houses without ventilation or fresh air.

Such conditions encouraged infectious diseases such as typhus, typhoid and cholera, and it was no surprise that many sought escape in the bottle. Drunkenness was endemic and the cause of much crime. The physical evidence of such low life disappeared long ago, but spare a thought for those who suffered the awful misery that lurked unseen along the river edge.

Address Blackfriars Bridge, Manchester M3 5NA | **Getting there** Tram (most lines) or train to Victoria and 10-minute walk | **Hours** Accessible 24 hours | **Tip** Walk along the river to the Trinity footbridge designed by the engineer Santiago Calatrava. Completed in 1995, it is his only work in the UK.

16 The Boulder in the Quad
When the Lake District came to Manchester

An enormous boulder sits on the lawn in a peaceful ivy-clad quadrangle of Manchester University. You'll find it by walking under the gothic archway in the old university buildings on Oxford Road and turning right. The gigantic stone is about nine feet high and weighs twenty tons. Geologically speaking, it is an andesite – a solidified lump of volcanic lava or magma formed when the magma erupts to the surface and crystallises quickly into a fine-grained rock. The name derives from the Andes, the mountain range in South America, where this type of rock was originally discovered, but andesite is found in volcanic zones all over the world. The Manchester boulder originated closer to home – it comes from Borrowdale. About 20,000 years ago, during the last Ice Age, the boulder was formed by volcanic activity in what is now the Lake District, and was carried by the movement of glaciers about 80 miles southwards. Glaciers move slowly and the boulder probably took a few hundred years to get there – a journey that now takes about two hours on the M6.

In 1888, excavations were taking place just south of the university building, on the corner of Oxford Road and Devas Street, probably in connection with the installation of sewers. The boulder was found 28 feet below the surface, craned out of the ground on a specially built wooden hoist, and transported the short distance to the university quadrangle on a railway trolley running on a makeshift track. In the archive of the first curator of the Manchester Museum there are sepia photographs recording the move, showing bowler-hatted workers proudly standing in front of the boulder, and some on top of it. The boulder is secured to the trolley with thick ropes, and there is a helmeted policeman on duty to keep bystanders away. It was quite a sensation at the time, but today most people walk past without noticing it.

Address Old Quadrangle, University of Manchester, Oxford Road, Manchester M13 9PL | **Getting there** Bus 41, 42, 43, 142, 143 or 147 to Manchester Museum | **Tip** As you exit the quad, look across Oxford Road and you will see the Sun high up on the opposite building. It's a sculpture by Lyn Chadwick, dating from 1963, and made of fibreglass coated in gold leaf.

17 Bridgewater Basin
Aquatic urban oasis

The Bridgewater Basin is a disused branch of the Rochdale Canal outside the Bridgewater Hall, just below the *Ishinki Touchstone* sculpture by Kan Yasuda. Neglected for years, the basin was choked with litter and weeds until imaginative thinking transformed it into an attractive and colourful water garden. The City Council worked with the Bridgewater Hall, the Canal and River Trust and other bodies, and now the misty spray of a fountain provides a backdrop for miniature islands of plants floating on the water. The stone steps leading down to the canal basin are a pleasant place to sit for a lunchtime sandwich on sunny days, and on warm evenings concert-goers mill around in the area overlooking the water.

According to the designers, the garden was inspired by the idea of musical composition, combining textures, shapes and movement: weeping willows and reeds sway in the background while the foreground planting gives vivid bursts of colour and spectacle. The choice of plants also suggests synaesthesia – a neurological phenomenon in which different sounds are associated with particular colours. An information panel quotes Kandinsky's view that 'Colour is the keyboard, the eyes are the harmonies, the soul is the piano with many strings,' and the composer Joachim Raff: 'the sound of a flute produced the sensation of intense azure blue; of the [oboe], yellow; cornet, green; trumpet, scarlet; the French horn purple; and the [bassoon] grey.'

If this all sounds too airy-fairy, the ecological benefits of the scheme are more convincing. The floating islands of plants encourage wildlife, providing safe havens for birds and insects, while the submerged roots give shelter to fish and encourage micro-organisms that break down pollution. Most people, however, will just enjoy the water garden for what it is – a haven of greenery in an area of stone, concrete and glass.

Address Lower Mosley Street, Manchester M2 3WS | Getting there Tram to St Peter's Square (all lines) | Hours Accessible 24 hours | Tip The brick building beyond the water garden was the warehouse of Sam Mendel, one of Manchester's wealthiest Victorian merchants. His business crashed when the Suez Canal opened and his paintings and furniture were auctioned by Christie's in a sale lasting 21 days.

18 Britannia Hotel (formerly Watts Warehouse)
Domain of a merchant prince

James Watts was a classic Manchester entrepreneur. He was the son of a self-made man, a free-trader and a dissenter, twice Lord Mayor of Manchester and later High Sheriff of Lancaster. He was concerned not only with business success, but also to make a social mark, and this spectacular warehouse built in the 1850s was a fitting statement for the owner of the city's largest wholesale drapery business. Watts' big moment came in 1857 when he entertained Prince Albert, who stayed at his sumptuous county house in Cheshire while visiting the Manchester Art Treasures Exhibition. There Watts liked to point to the verse from *Proverbs* on his library ceiling 'Seest thou a man diligent in his business, He shall stand before kings' and recount that he had not stood but sat beneath it while speaking to the Prince.

As with most of Manchester's large warehouses, Watts Warehouse was used not just for storage of cotton goods, but included showrooms, offices, areas for quality control, preparation and packing. Instead of having utilitarian façades, it was designed to evoke the palaces of 16th-century Italy. Yet within an Italianate framework, Watts' architects, Travis and Mangnall, could not resist showing off their command of architectural history by giving each floor a different style: Italian Renaissance, Elizabethan, French Renaissance and Flemish, with Gothic at the top. The building had to impress buyers from across the world, and once inside the visitor ascended a magnificent cast-iron staircase with spacious landings, to inspect the goods. The warehouse narrowly avoided demolition when it closed in 1972, later becoming a hotel. Notwithstanding the chequered reputation of the Britannia Hotel chain, the building's present brashness and glitter is well suited to its status as the queen of Manchester warehouses.

Address Portland Street, Manchester M1 3LA, +44 (0)781 222 0017, www.britanniahotels.com/hotels/the-britannia-hotel-manchester | Getting there Tram (most lines) or bus to Piccadilly Gardens | Tip The finest group of commercial warehouses in the city is on nearby Princess Street where block after block of impressive palazzo-style buildings of regular height and proportion stretch into the distance.

19 Bury Market
Black pudding and Chorley cakes

Until the supermarkets killed them off, there used to be markets in every suburb of Manchester as well as all the surrounding towns. Of those that remain, Bury is the biggest and best, bustling and colourful with over 350 stalls in the market halls and the open air selling everything under the sun from fruit and vegetables to jam, jigsaw puzzles and pet food, with traders who love to chat, and an array of cafés serving traditional fry-ups, fish and chips or falafel. In the open market, Harry Muffin's sells the largest scones you have ever seen, Chorley cakes the size of dinner plates, fat Eccles cakes and whinberry pies (whinberry is the local name for bilberry).

Nearby are the vendors of black pudding, synonymous with Bury market – two rival makers compete for custom. The Bury Black Pudding Company boasts 'the only black pudding made in Bury,' while Chadwick's Original Bury Black Puddings claims a secret recipe dating back to 1865 and names Prince Charles and the late Ken Dodd as customers. You can buy it fat or lean, gluten-free and, believe it or not, in a vegetarian version substituting black beans for the pig's blood and pork fat that, for *aficionados*, gives the local delicacy its 'pure porcine perfection'.

Black puddings are also on sale in the modern metal and glass Fish and Meat Hall, with its tempting abundance of glistening fish, Goosnargh poultry and meats including rare breeds from farms in Lancashire, Cheshire and Cumbria, laid out on long stainless-steel counters. This is the liveliest part of the market, with the butchers calling out their wares and joshing with customers: 'Buy a big tray of steak, get your chicken free,' shouts the butcher's boy from Brandwood's while another offers '40 quid's worth of meat for 25,' adding to general laughter 'I'm not here to break the bank, I'm here to make friends.' Shopping doesn't have to be sterile supermarket aisles and checkout queues, and Bury market is the proof.

Address 1 Murray Road, Bury BL9 0BJ, www.burymarket.com | **Getting there** Tram to Bury (Bury line) | **Hours** Market Hall temporarily closed, check website for update; Fish and Meat Market Mon, Wed–Sat 9am–4.30pm, Tue 9am–noon; Open Market Wed & Fri 9am–4.30pm, Sat 9am–5pm | **Tip** In Library Gardens (7-minute walk) is a statue of local comedian Victoria Wood.

20 Castlefield Railway Viaducts
The march of the giants

During the 19th century, the Castlefield area was sliced up by successive transport networks. First came the canals and later the railways, and where they crossed, the rail tracks were lifted up on massive viaducts that smashed through the densely populated area.

Both the Bridgewater and Rochdale Canals terminate at the Castlefield Basin, where early warehouses and canal structures still stand. In 1830 the Liverpool to Manchester Railway arrived with the opening of the world's first passenger railway station at Liverpool Road; followed in 1849 by the Manchester, South Junction and Altrincham Railway that built a huge brick viaduct with skewed iron bridges crossing the Rochdale Canal. But the most ruthless construction was the approach to Central Station when over 1,200 people, among the poorest and most vulnerable in the town, lost their homes. The perpetrator was the Cheshire Lines Committee, a railway conglomerate that came together to build this heroic project in the 1870s and added another viaduct in 1893. The giant legs of the iron and steel viaducts marched across the canal network to reach the city centre. Remains of the Roman fort were smashed in the process, the shattered fragments referenced by dressing up the viaducts with turrets and castellations. The culmination was the construction of the Great Northern Goods Warehouse in 1898, which provided an interchange between rail, canal and road. The railway came in on yet another viaduct with access from street level via ramps fitted with hydraulic haulage, and hoists down to the Manchester and Salford Junction Canal that runs in a tunnel beneath the building. The warehouse has been converted into a leisure complex and one of the redundant viaducts is being transformed as a New York Highline-style park by the National Trust.

Address Castle Street, Manchester M3 4LZ | **Getting there** Tram to Deansgate/Castlefield (all lines) and 5-minute walk | **Hours** National Trust viaduct free walk-up visits Wed–Sun 10am–5pm, castlefieldviaduct@nationaltrust.org.uk | **Tip** The recently completed Ordsall Chord, connecting a number of the viaducts, has revealed for the first time in 150 years the Stephenson Bridge that led into the terminus of the world's first passenger railway.

21   Cathedral Choir
'Rabbit's Revenge'

Manchester Cathedral's great treasure is the magnificent woodwork of the choir. The choir stalls that surround it on three sides, carved with expert skill, have two tiers of canopies bristling with spiky finials, the upper row pierced to look like miniature Gothic windows. Above is a tester, a kind of projecting fascia with shallow arches. Even more elaborate carving is on the Dean's and Canons' stalls, backing onto the rood screen that separates the choir from the nave.

Also worth admiring are the bench and desk ends. The latter incorporate tiny buildings with gables and tiled roofs, and above are beasts, whose hind quarters rest on the curved sweep of the stall end. The choir stalls were installed around 1500, paid for by Richard Beswick, a wealthy merchant, and James Stanley, a local aristocrat who later became Bishop of Ely. The stalls are similar in style to those at Ripon and Beverley Minsters, and are amongst the finest in the north of England.

Most engaging are the 30 misericords or backs of the seats, so named after the Latin word for 'pity', for when tipped up they provide support for the worshipper when required to stand. They are carved with a host of charming, cartoon-like scenes. Look out for the wild men fighting on camel and unicorn; the pedlar robbed by monkeys; and the piglets dancing to bagpipes played by the sow, all on the south side. On the opposite side, you can seek out the woman scolding her husband for breaking the cooking pot; and the two men playing backgammon. Everyone's favourite is 'Rabbit's Revenge' showing the rabbit which, having captured the hunter and his dog, cooks them for dinner. The grand bishop's chair or cathedra, marked by the bishop's coat of arms, only dates from 1906, but it too includes a strange animal – a kangaroo – which would have tickled the fancy of the medieval carvers had they seen it.

Address Victoria Street, Manchester M3 1SX, +44 (0)161 833 2220, www.manchestercathedral.org | **Getting there** Tram (most lines) or train to Victoria and 5-minute walk | **Hours** Mon–Sat 9.30am–4pm, Sun noon–4pm (times may vary during special events) | **Tip** Over the entrance to the Chapter House is a curious painting by Carel Weight showing Jesus preaching with scenes of the blessed set in modern times.

22 Central Ref
Therefore get wisdom

When Manchester Central Reference Library reopened in 2014 after a four-year closure for refurbishment, the press releases trumpeted digital this and interactive that. Superfast broadband, 200 computers stuffed with the latest software, a Mediathèque showing films and TV shows, a Business Library equipped to support the entrepreneurs of the future, three lifts, five new entrances, glass walls, open-plan study areas and 2,000 metres of extra lending space. All this plus a café serving Lancashire crisps and Manchester fruit cake – but what about the books? They didn't rate a mention.

Architect Vincent Harris' circular Portland Stone building, opened in 1943, had certainly become shabby, its layout confusing, its one lift an embarrassment and its services inadequate. The renovation is a triumph – and the books are still there.

The one space that did not need bells and whistles has been treated with appropriate restraint: the circular Reading Room. The clutter of card catalogues and filing cabinets has gone and the magnificently simple lines of Harris' design revealed once again: the yellow Tuscan columns, the broad dome and the central desk (now no longer used for issuing books) with its spherical clock floating above rococo scrolls. Even the famously deafening echo has been softened.

Millions of students have spent hours here, revising or researching, seated on the spacious wooden chairs at the long tables with their built-in reading lights, all beautifully restored. As is the quotation from Proverbs running round the dome – 'Wisdom is the principal thing; therefore get wisdom, and with all thy getting get understanding. Exalt her and she shall promote thee; she shall bring thee to honour when thou dost embrace her, she shall give of thine head an ornament of grace, a crown of glory she shall deliver to thee.' Still there to inspire the students of the future.

Address St Peter's Square, Manchester M2 5PD, +44 (0)161 234 1983, www.manchester.gov.uk/centrallibrary | **Getting there** Tram to St Peter's Square (all lines) | **Hours** Mon–Thu 9am–8pm, Fri & Sat 9am–5pm | **Tip** Home, Tony Wilson Square, Manchester's centre for contemporary arts, includes what used to be the Library Theatre, which moved out of Central Ref in order to maximise library space.

23 Chinese Garden at RHS Bridgewater
Painting a picture in plants

At the heart of the new Bridgewater Gardens that opened in May 2021 is the Chinese Streamside Garden, a collaboration between Salford's Chinese community, horticultural experts in China and the Royal Horticultural Society. RHS Bridgewater is one of Europe's largest garden projects, and marks a new approach for the RHS in restoring a historic landscape that was abandoned 70 years ago. While some traces of the original gardens remained, such as the magnificent walled garden and the lake, the RHS chose to create 'a new painting in the historic frame', combining restoration with new landscapes designed by Tom Stuart Smith.

Covering seven acres, the Chinese Streamside Garden features a meandering stream connecting the upper Ellesmere Lake with Moon Bridge Water, a new lake that takes its name from an ancient Chinese poem. It has been designed by the Chinese landscape expert Fan Xuquan who has taken inspiration from the Ye Garden in his city, Yangzhou, to represent a mountain scene. The rocks have been arranged to represent miniature mountain peaks, artfully combined with plants chosen for their texture and colour to create a scene as if in a Chinese painting. At the head of the stream is a large pool, from which the water gently falls via a succession of cascades, smaller pools and weirs. Visitors weave their way along the sinuous path through woodland, a bamboo garden and a Chinese meadow, crossing the stream over five wooden bridges. On display are many of the UK's favourite plants that originate from China: magnolias, rhododendrons, hydrangeas, primula, *Ginko Biloba* and the beautiful handkerchief tree *Davidia Involucrata*. It reminds us of the immense contribution made to British horticulture by the introduction of Chinese plants.

Address Worsley New Hall, Occupation Road, off Leigh Road, Worsley M28 2LJ, +44 (0)161 503 6100, www.rhs.org.uk/gardens/bridgewater | **Getting there** Bus 35 from Piccadilly Gardens to Occupation Road and 10-minute walk | **Hours** Nov–Feb daily 10am–4pm; Mar–Oct daily 10am–6pm | **Tip** Worsley Old Hall off Old Hall Lane is a traditional pub with good hearty food. The house dates from the early 17th century but was substantially rebuilt in the Victorian period for members of the Egerton family.

24 Chorlton Water Park
Grebes, bats and hula hoops

The River Mersey begins its journey in Stockport, fed by tributaries that gush down from the rain-soaked Pennine Hills. It then meanders through a wide flood plain that bisects the southern suburbs of Manchester, before collecting the Rivers Irk and Medlock to finally become the mighty watercourse that meets the sea at Liverpool. In those flood plains, just five short miles from the city centre, is Chorlton Water Park, Manchester's first designated nature reserve.

Covering 170 acres, its centrepiece is a lake that was formed by flooding a gravel pit excavated for the construction of the M60 motorway. From the lakeside, a footbridge over the Mersey leads to woodland and meadows traversed by winding paths, where ponds and marshy areas provide habitats for wildlife. Well before the lake was created, when this land belonged to Barlow Hall Farm (now Chorlton Golf Clubhouse), it was deliberately flooded in the winter months. As the water receded in spring, it left a layer of rich silt that produced abundant grasses that were cut for hay in late summer. Although the system of sluices and drainage ditches that controlled the water has now mostly been lost, the semi-natural grasslands on both sides of the river still retain a wide range of species associated with ancient water meadows.

The water park is also home to more than 65 types of birds, including swans, cormorants, great crested grebe and other waterfowl. Bullfinches, chaffinches, redwing and wrens flit back and forth, while high overhead buzzards soar and kestrels hover. A heron stands motionless on the water's edge awaiting a passing fish, and at dusk the rare Daubenton's bat ventures out of the woods. On your circuit of the lake you will meet dog walkers, anglers, joggers and you may even get a sighting of Pramactive – a local group of young mums keeping fit with hula hoops, their babies in tow.

Address Maitland Avenue, Manchester M21 7WH | **Getting there** Tram to Sale Water Park (navy line) and 15-minute walk along River Mersey | **Hours** Accessible 24 hours | **Tip** Still on a watery theme, The Oystercatcher at 123 Manchester Road, Chorlton-cum-Hardy is among the city's best seafood restaurants.

25 Closing Cotton Prices at the Royal Exchange
The end of an era

The Royal Exchange was the focus of Manchester's commercial life for almost 250 years until the building closed its doors on 31 December, 1968. Since then the global cotton prices for that final day have been frozen in time on the old trading board fixed high on the wall. In the late 19th century, the Exchange cornered 80 per cent of the world's finished cotton trade, and in the 1920s it was the largest place of assembly for trade in the world with 11,000 members. Twice weekly the Great Hall filled up with a vast throng of men in top hats or bowlers buying and selling cotton and everything associated with its production. The first Exchange opened in 1729, but 90 years later this was replaced by a new building, which was enlarged and then superseded by the present one to meet business demands. The final phase, including the imposing entrance from St Ann's Square, was completed in 1921, but the building's heyday was short lived. After serious damage in the Blitz, half the trading floor was closed off and converted to offices. Yet what remains today is still a gargantuan space, clad in coloured marble and lit by domes.

Closure of the trading floor in 1968 led to a new phase in the building's history. Today, the Great Hall is filled with the 'Lunar Module', a modern tubular steel theatre-in-the-round that hovers above the floor suspended from four main columns. Opened by Sir Laurence Olivier, and now more than 40 years old, this daring structure still has the power to shock. During those years, it has seen the likes of Tom Courtenay and Albert Finney, Vanessa Redgrave and Julie Walters, and the resident company continues to challenge and delight its audiences. Among all the theatrical glitter, the closing prices stand aloof as a reminder of the city's mercantile might in the years of the Industrial Revolution.

Address St Ann's Square, Manchester M2 7DH, +44 (0)161 833 9833, www.royalexchange.co.uk | **Getting there** Free bus (route 2) to Market Street or tram (most lines) to Exchange Square Check website for show times and tickets | **Tip** The other great city centre commodities exchange to survive is the Corn Exchange of 1903 on Corporation Street, now a place of restaurants and bars.

26 Contact Theatre
The face of carbon zero

The huge quirky chimneys that rise like a Heath Robinson rocket launcher over the sprawling university campus along Oxford Road signal that here is a building that does things differently. When constructed in the late '90s, the Contact Theatre was the first naturally ventilated theatre in the UK with an exceptionally low carbon footprint. Its architect Alan Short was a pioneer of sustainable design and now, after recent refurbishment and extension, the theatre's performance puts it in the top 1% of the most environmentally friendly public buildings in the north-west. The chimneys, which allow fresh air to flow naturally through the building, are supplemented by sophisticated monitoring and control systems that minimize heat loss in winter and provide night cooling in summer. LED technology, full daylighting of internal working spaces and a kill switch to ensure that all lights are switched off by the last person out are some of the other energy-saving devices.

Founded as the Manchester Young People's Theatre 50 years ago, Contact's mission to help young people from all backgrounds to act as creative leaders and agents of social change has led to its success. Not only does this mean that half of its Board of Trustees are under 30 and its chair is 28, but that the building reflects the attitudes of its members, staff and audience. This includes the emphasis on sustainability, the bright pink and yellow colours that animate the interior, and its progressive spirit, all of which foster engagement with the arts. Dance, music, poetry, spoken word, hip hop and art combine with traditional theatre to spark inspiration. The relaxed vibe of the bar and café, Brew, with coffee from local roastery ManCoCo, signals that this is not just a place for performance, but for meeting, eating and hanging out. Devotees of this remarkable building hail it as Gaudi come to Manchester.

Address Contact Theatre, Oxford Road, Manchester M15 6JA, www.contactmcr.com; Box Office: boxoffice@contactmcr.com | **Getting there** Bus 41, 42, 43, 143 or 147 to Manchester University | **Hours** Tue–Fri 9am–8pm, plus special events, see website | **Tip** Another university building that is famed for innovation is the National Graphene Institute on Booth Street East, a hotbed of research into how graphene can change the world.

27   The Curry Mile
India on a plate

Brightly lit garish plastic fascias, spicy aromas wafting into the street, cheap curries that burn your insides, bumper-to-bumper traffic jams: the stretch of Wilmslow Road at Rusholme used to be the biggest concentration of South Asian restaurants outside the Indian subcontinent. No longer: many places have closed, and shisha bars, kebab houses and Middle Eastern restaurants have moved in along with Turkish barbers, Syrian cake shops and Halal supermarkets full of exotic-looking vegetables. But it is still fun to wander about and mingle with the crowds in the early evening and to peer into the lighted shop windows full of saris, glistening jewellery and Indian wedding outfits heavy with gold embroidery and precious stones; or the shops selling mithai – luridly coloured Indian and Pakistani sweets cut into diamond and square shapes and piled up in architectural compositions.

Cheapo formica counters and fluorescent tubes are still in evidence at the takeaways and smaller cafés, but the more upmarket places have realised the need to move with the times or go under. They compete for custom with eye-catching décor – chandeliers, waterfalls and giant TV sets showing sport and Bollywood musicals. Food styles have also been updated: fusion menus offer pasta, pizza and Halal burgers alongside the usual masalas, kormas and jalfrezis. For the best eating, head for Mughli Charcoal Pit, an established favourite on the Mile, serving authentic curries and tandoori dishes inspired by the street food and family kitchens of Mughal India. If you prefer something more contemporary, try Ziya Asian Grill for a sophisticated modern take on Indian cooking, stylishly presented in elegant surroundings. Just avoid the area after 1am, when buses and taxis from the city centre begin to disgorge crowds of tanked-up youngsters in search of a cheap curry after a night of clubbing.

Address Wilmslow Road between Great Western Street and Dickenson Road, Rusholme, Manchester M14 5TQ | **Getting there** Bus 41, 42, 43, 142, 143 or 147 to Rusholme | **Tip** For a more sedate old-style curry house, try the Great Kathmandu at 140 Burton Road, Didsbury, serving award-winning Nepalese and Indian food.

28 Dale Street
Filming the Big Apple

If you want to know what the rougher parts of New York looked like in the 1940s, go to Dale Street in the Northern Quarter. Textile warehouses from the Victorian and Edwardian period line the street and the narrow alleyways leading off it, complete with granite cobbles, goods hoists and iron escape stairs. Because the buildings remain so intact, the street and others around have frequently been used as film sets.

In 2011, Dale Street was transformed into downtown Manhattan for the blockbuster Marvel movie *Captain America: the First Avenger*. The stretch between Port Street and Lena Street was dressed up for the dramatic escape after the treacherous Kruger, played by Richard Armitage, makes off with a sample of the body-enhancing formula from the secret lab lurking inside Brooklyn Antiques. 1940s Chevrolets and Studebakers brought over from the States were the stars of the high-speed car chase.

Nearby High Street also featured as the Big Apple in the 2004 remake of *Alfie* starring Jude Law as the charming British philanderer who cruises the streets as a limousine chauffeur. For the film, a café was specially built at the corner with Soap Street. Jude Law came back to the Northern Quarter along with Colin Firth and Nicole Kidman in 2016 for a shoot of the film *Genius*. Set in 1900s New York, this tells the story of literary editor Max Perkins, who helped to shape novels by some of America's most famous writers including Ernest Hemingway and F. Scott Fitzgerald. More recently, and without any dressing up, Dale Street was much in evidence in the brilliantly comic and often poignant Channel 4 TV drama *Cucumber* about Manchester's gay scene by the writer and director of *Queer as Folk*, Russell T. Davies, while nearby Paton Street was used in his award-winning *It's a Sin*. So take a stroll down to Dale Street and you might end up with a walk-on part in a TV show or Hollywood movie.

Address Dale Street, Manchester M1 1JB | **Getting there** 4–minute walk from Piccadilly Gardens | **Tip** Corporation Street and Cannon Street before the construction of the Arndale Centre feature in the cult classic *Hell is a City*, starring Stanley Baker and Billie Whitelaw, which was almost wholly shot in Manchester.

29 Deadstock General Store
Retail is detail

'Hats, Bags and Fancy Goods' announces the sign on the window; peer into Deadstock General Store, and you will see an idiosyncratic collection of things useful – hot water bottles, scissors, watering cans, wooden brushes – and beautiful, like the delicate botanical specimens suspended in resin from Usagi no Nedoko of Kyoto or the delightfully eccentric ceramics by Studio Arhoj of Copenhagen. This small shop was created by Liam Jackson, a fashion graduate of Manchester Met and the Royal College of Art. In 2013 he returned from London and, judging that there weren't any interesting shops in Manchester, he opened one of his own.

The interior is simple, lined in wood, with an antique cash register on the counter. For his stock, which is anything but dead, Liam chooses the kind of things he would be happy to have in his own home. 'We are very particular about what we stock and source our products from all over the world, with a focus on classic and well-designed goods.' The range constantly evolves and you can check out the new arrivals on Liam's Bindle Store website.

Liam has an eye for cult brands, such as Mauna Keya, Japanese makers of comfy hemp and cotton socks. He loves design classics such as chunky Kaweco 'Sport' pens from Germany, laid out in rows to show off the many colours. Toiletries include Marvis, a sought-after Italian toothpaste in extraordinary flavours, like Jasmine Mint, Liquorice or Orange-blossom; kelp-based skincare products by Haeckels of Margate; and Swedish fragrances inspired by Swedish folklore from niche perfumery Stora Skuggan. Stylish berets are by the German brand Kopka, and you can also buy combs made of recycled plastic in a range of marbled colours. In winter, the shop sells fluffy slippers, scarves and gloves; in summer sunglasses and straw hats; and, this being Manchester, Liam stocks very special EuroSCHIRM high-performance umbrellas all year round.

Address 48 Edge Street, Manchester M4 1HN, +44(0)792 557 7054, www.bindlestore.com, liam@deadstockgeneralstore.com | Getting there Tram (most lines) to Shudehill and 4-minute walk | Hours Mon–Sat 11am–6pm, Sun noon–5pm | Tip Liam's favourite eatery is The Pasta Factory, run by foodies from Turin who make fresh pasta daily. Enjoy it in their restaurant at 77 Shudehill or buy some to cook at home.

30 Dormouse Chocolates
Manchester's first bean to bar

Warning! Dairy Milk fans or Mars Bar addicts, this place is not for you. Dormouse Chocolate is nothing like mass-market brands – it is handmade from single-estate beans selected for their complex flavours. Made with less sugar than factory-produced chocolate, it is high in cocoa solids (you can buy a 100 per cent bar if you dare). This is chocolate to be savoured like wine: no munching and definitely no bingeing. It has won top national and international awards and is sold at gourmet chocolate stores all over the world.

The genius behind Dormouse is Isobel Carse, a former law student whose life changed direction when she took a Christmas job as a shop assistant at Hotel Chocolat. Promoted to the chocolate-making side of the business, she stayed with the company for several years before setting up on her own, at first working from home, and is now based in premises just off Deansgate. Her beans are sourced from small producers through ethical co-operatives to ensure fair prices. Starting with the raw beans, she roasts, pounds and mixes, adding unrefined sugar and organic milk as required. She tempers the resulting paste for a glossy finish, moulds it into bars and finally wraps the bars in the beautiful handmade papers that are the brand's signature.

Dormouse is open to visitors on four afternoons a week, when Isobel will talk chocolate with you, offering samples from tiny copper bowls to help you choose. Will it be the Guatemala 51.5 per cent milk chocolate or the Madagascar 75.6 per cent dark? Besides making single-estate bars, she loves experimenting with novel taste combinations – try the raspberry and almond, or the toasted white chocolate, or her Christmas specials flavoured with stollen or speculaas (Dutch spice biscuits). If you still can't decide, you can always join the Bean to Door Club and receive a limited-edition bar each month.

Address Unit 0, Deansgate Mews, Great Northern Warehouse, Manchester M3 4EN, +44 (0)739 802 0328, www.dormousechocolates.co.uk | **Getting there** Tram to Deansgate-Castlefield (all lines) | **Hours** Wed & Thu noon–2pm, Fri noon–4pm, Sat 10am–4pm | **Tip** Take the lift up to Cloud 23, the bar on the 23rd floor of the Hilton Hotel, almost next door, and enjoy the fabulous view while relaxing with a drink.

31 East Lancashire Railway
Steaming ahead

Dressed in peaked cap and three-piece suit, complete with watch chain and whiskers, the friendly station guard blows his whistle, and with a long hiss of steam the 11.30 for Ramsbottom moves off. If you remember the days of steam, the East Lancashire Railway will be for you, and if you don't, you will wish you did.

The railway between Heywood and Rawtenstall was a casualty of Dr Beeching's destructive axe in the 1960s when many branch lines were closed. In the Rossendale Valley, the local community never accepted the loss of their train service, and in 1987 the East Lancashire Railway Preservation Trust reopened the line between Bury and Ramsbottom, gradually extending it in both directions. Two new bridges were built and the volunteer-run railway now attracts 150,000 passengers a year. Some come for a day out in the country and others to feast on board, with afternoon tea or a five-course meal in the luxurious dining car. You can join a steam-powered real ale tour of the valleys' best pubs and bars, including the Buffer Stops at Rawtenstall, or why not fulfil your childhood dream and spend a day learning to drive one of the gleaming locomotives?

The railway passes through some beautiful countryside, stopping at local stations where you can get off the train to explore the villages before hopping on the next one that passes. Some stations are suitably equipped with vintage weighing machines, milk churns, sacks of potatoes and porters' trolleys stacked with trunks.

Across the Road from Bury Station is the Trust's Museum, where you can see steam engines, the earliest an 1881 shunter; and a collection of diesel engines, most of which are from the 1960s. In summer, everyone's favourite blue locomotive, Thomas the Tank Engine, comes into service accompanied by the Fat Controller and the Troublesome Trucks. As a journey back in time it takes some beating.

Address Bury Bolton Street Station, Bolton Street, Bury BL9 0EY, +44 (0)333 320 2830, www.eastlancsrailway.org.uk | **Getting there** Tram to Bury (Bury line) | **Hours** Apr–Sept Wed–Sun, Oct–Mar Sat & Sun, also bank holidays and special occasions; see website for train times | **Tip** Walk up the hill from Ramsbottom Station to Market Place to see Edward Allington's bronze sculpture *Tilted Vase* pouring water into a hole in the pavement; it celebrates the town's place on the River Irwell.

32   Edgar Wood in Middleton
Artistry in architecture

As a young man growing up in the unremarkable mill town of Middleton, Edgar Wood fell under the influence of William Morris. Wood trained as an architect and became a keen advocate of the Arts and Crafts Movement. His early buildings have an exaggerated geometry that makes them highly expressionistic, with steeply sloping roofs and contrasting textures of brick, stone and roughcast. He went on to design houses in a more austere style with flat reinforced-concrete roofs, plain brickwork and simple geometric decoration. Far in advance of his contemporaries, he is now hailed as a pioneer of modern architecture.

The key building in Middleton is the Long Street Methodist Church of 1901, from where you can take a short walk up the main road to see six more of Wood's works. The tall church and the lower school and hall form three sides of a garden courtyard, with an eye-catching Gothic archway and distinctive window tracery on the street front. Across the road in Jubilee Gardens is a semi-circular stone staircase designed as the setting for a now lost fountain. Further on, at the corner with Cleworth Road, is an asymmetrical pair of houses from 1895, Fencegate and Redcroft – the latter was Wood's own house – both with attractive gateways and front gardens. Just beyond the next turning is another pair, 51–53 Rochdale Road, more regular in stone and brick, but with subtle differences in the design of the bays. Retracing your steps, be sure not to miss 1 Towncroft Avenue of 1901, which marks the start of Wood's cubic style with flat concrete roofs front and back. Then at 36 Mellalieu Street is a true statement of modernism from 1906, complete with expanded-metal fence, a replica of Wood's original design. Finally, the pub, formerly a bank, at the bottom of Long Street is an early work of 1892, clad in pink terracotta with eccentric Art Nouveau downpipes.

Address Long Street Methodist Church, 93 Long Street, Middleton M24 6UN, www.artsandcraftschurch.org | **Getting there** Bus 117 from Shudehill to Cemetery Street, Middleton | **Hours** The church is open for services Sun 11am; for visits by appointment contact edgarwoodsociety@gmail.com | **Tip** Close to the church in Long Street is the Olde Boar's Head, an ancient inn serving traditional pub food. The building was saved from demolition by a campaign started by Wood.

33 Egyptian Tomb
Journey into the netherworld

It comes as a surprise to most people that Bolton Museum has an important Egyptian collection – a staggering 12,000 objects including colourful textiles, jewellery, amulets, alabaster jars and a gorgeously painted mummy case. The story of how all these items came to Bolton starts in the Victorian era when the town's mills imported large amounts of cotton from Egypt. Annie Barlow, the daughter of one of the principal mill owners, became interested in Egypt and helped to raise money for excavations. Donors were allocated a share of the finds, and Barlow gave hers to the local museum, working with the curators to build a collection. Today, Bolton's Egyptian galleries are spectacular: you walk through a series of glass cases, with artefacts shown overhead as well as at the sides – a vivid panorama that illustrates the way of life and the funeral customs of the ancient Egyptians.

The most remarkable item is a full-size walk-in replica of the burial chamber of Pharaoh Thutmose III from the Valley of the Kings. A military genius, he created the largest empire Egypt had ever known. The facsimile of his tomb was made using laser technology and finished by hand with cracks and chips to reproduce the effects of 3,500 years of ageing. All around are wall paintings of stick figures enacting the Pharaoh's hazardous journey through the underworld over the 12 hours of darkness after his burial. An engaging short animated film explains the different stages of the journey, which ends at sunrise when the dead ruler was reborn to become at one with the sun god Ra. It is quite spooky, as in the tomb there is a real mummy, blackened and shrivelled – it isn't Thutmose, however, but an unknown man, possibly a priest. Bolton does have a piece of linen from the wrappings of the Pharaoh's corpse and a painted block from his tomb but Thutmose's mummy rests in the Cairo Museum.

Address Bolton Museum, Le Mans Crescent, Bolton BL1 1SE, +44 (0)120 433 2211, www.boltonlams.co.uk | Getting there Train to Bolton | Hours Mon, Tue, Thu–Sat 9am–5pm, Wed 9.30am–5pm, Sun 10.30am–4.30pm | Tip Another tale of death: in 1651 the 7th Earl of Derby was beheaded outside Ye Olde Man and Scythe in Churchgate. The chair that he sat on prior to his execution is displayed inside the pub, with a wax head and an axe.

34 Elizabeth Gaskell's House
Victorian literary life

The novelist Elizabeth Gaskell was born in Chelsea, but after her mother died she was brought up by an aunt in Knutsford. In 1842 she married Revd William Gaskell, Minister of the Unitarian Cross Street Chapel, Manchester. They started a family and in 1853 moved into 84 Plymouth Grove, a handsome classical villa with 20 rooms. Many well-to-do Mancunians lived in houses like this, but almost all of them have been demolished. At that time the area was still a semi-rural suburb – the house had larger gardens than at present, where the Gaskells kept chickens, ducks, pigs, a pony and a cow.

Elizabeth lived here until her death in 1865. While she was at Plymouth Grove she wrote several of her most famous books including *Cranford*, based on life in Knutsford, *Ruth*, about a poor seamstress who became an unmarried mother, and *North and South*, her second Manchester novel. Like her first novel, *Mary Barton*, it was based on her sympathetic observation of the grim lives of Manchester factory workers. During these years, Mrs Gaskell also enjoyed a busy social life – her husband was one of Manchester's leading Unitarians, involved with many local causes and societies, and she had many of her literary friends to stay including Charles Dickens, Charlotte Brontë, Harriet Beecher Stowe and John Ruskin. At the same time, Mrs Gaskell brought up four daughters – one of them had piano lessons from Charles Hallé.

The house fell on hard times in the 1990s but was restored with charitable funds including the National Lottery and reopened in 2014. Although few items now in the house were owned by the Gaskells, Victorian furniture and colour schemes, specially woven textiles and books of the period have been used to create convincing interiors of the 1860s. It is ironic that after the last of the Gaskells died in 1913 the house was offered to the council as a museum – and turned down.

Address 84 Plymouth Grove, Manchester M13 9LW, +44 (0)161 273 2215, www.elizabethgaskellhouse.co.uk | **Getting there** Bus 197 to Hyde Road or 50 to Swinton Grove and 5-minute walk | **Hours** Wed, Thu & Sun 11am–4.30pm | **Tip** A 10-minute walk away is Daisy Bank Road, where you can see the First Church of Christ Scientist by the Middleton architect Edgar Wood, one of the most original buildings of its date (1904) and still an extraordinary sight.

35 Ellenroad Engine House
The world's biggest working steam engine

The huge Ellenroad Spinning Mill was built alongside the River Beal in the 1880s. Now only the Engine House is left, but the engine inside is a marvel of the age. Created by John McNaught of Rochdale, it was modified to achieve greater power following a fire in 1916 when the mill was rebuilt to house more modern machinery. It continued to run until 1975, by which time it had become the last of the great steam engines to drive a working mill and was saved by a trust with the support of the owners and Rochdale Council. Since then the trust has acquired other engines and mechanical equipment to add to its growing collection.

On steaming days, the great engine on the upper floor is brought into action by a band of volunteers. First, coal is shovelled by hand into the mechanical stokers feeding the two furnaces of the Lancashire boiler below. Fans supply air, which raises the temperature of the fuel, and 6,000 gallons of water are drawn off the river each minute to condense the steam used in the giant cylinders. Up above, tension rises as Victoria and Alexandra, the twin engines that work in tandem to turn the giant flywheel, are prepared: valves are checked, oil reservoirs are filled and casings are polished amidst the smell of hot oil and the gleam of brass and shining metal. The first movement is almost imperceptible, piston rods begin to slide slowly and silently, and pinion gears start to rotate. Then all of a sudden, the two queens speed up, the pistons swooshing forward and back with a rhythmic action, accompanied by gentle clicking and clacking of countless moving parts.

The great wheel is now rotating at a terrific rate, 58 revolutions a minute, providing the force that would have driven the spinning machines that occupied the five floors of the mill via the rope race and connecting shafts. Such is the power of this elegant and almost noiseless beauty.

Address Elizabeth Way, Newhey, Rochdale OL16 4LE, +44 (0)7981 391603, www.ellenroad.org.uk | **Getting there** Tram to Newhey (pink line) and 12-minute walk | **Hours** Steaming days are on the first Sunday of every month except January from 11am–4pm. Check the website in advance for future events | **Tip** The Bolton Steam Museum has a large collection of engines housed at Mornington Road, BL1 4EU; see www.nmes.org for opening times.

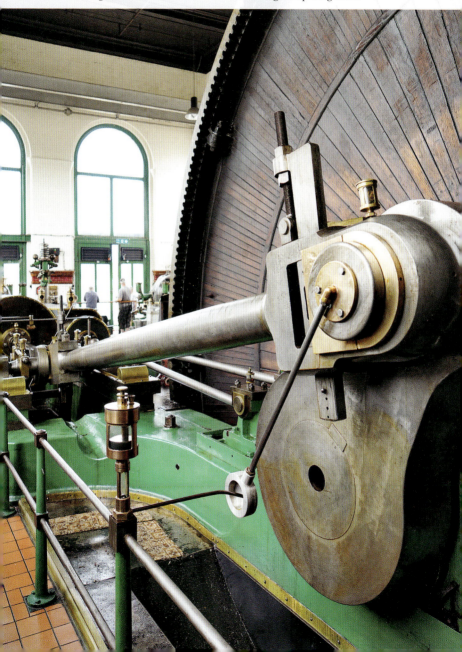

36 Engels' Beard
Radical facial hair

It could have fallen from a toppled statue, this colossal broken head with a luxuriant beard lying on the ground at Salford University; indeed, the idea for the sculpture came to the artist Jai Redman after reading about a plan to bring an unwanted statue of Engels over from the Soviet bloc in the 1980s. At the time it came to nothing, but the plan was realised much later in 2017 when a concrete statue of Engels from the Ukraine was transported across Europe and relocated in Tony Wilson Square outside the arts centre Home. In the meantime, Redman's idea was approved and his sculpture was installed in 2016.

Manchester's fascination with Engels comes from its history as a seedbed for radicalism. Both sculptures remind us of the role the city played in the evolution of Engels' thought: he was sent from Germany to Manchester at the age of 22 to work for his father's textile business, and while he was there observed the way of life in the slums of Salford and Manchester, collecting materials for his world-changing book *The Condition of the Working Class in England*.

The statue of Engels in Tony Wilson Square is a typically bland piece of Soviet propaganda showing Engels standing on a pedestal while the Salford work, which is made of fibreglass, is quite different – a wry celebration not a memorial, a metaphor not a portrait. The focus is not Engels' face but his beard because, according to Redman, beards are associated with wisdom and learning. Even more unusual is the fact that the sculpture is also a climbing wall – the idea of students clambering up it and 'standing on the shoulders of giants' is an appealing one (the quotation comes from Isaac Newton). *Engels' Beard* was criticised as kitsch and shallow when it was unveiled, but for most people it is a refreshing and witty reinterpretation of an outdated sculptural idiom – especially for those who climb up it.

Address Outside the New Adelphi building, Peel Park Campus, University Road, Salford M5 4BR | **Getting there** Train to Salford Crescent | **Hours** Accessible 24 hours | **Tip** Find out more about Engels in the Working Class Movement Library, based on the outstanding collection of Edmund and Ruth Frow, at nearby 51 The Crescent, Salford (open by appointment Tue–Fri 10am–4pm, and to drop-in visitors Wed–Fri 1–4.30pm).

37 esea contemporary
Small gallery, global reach

There is always something unusual to see in this beautifully designed gallery in part of the old Smithfield Market building in the Northern Quarter. ESEA stands for East and Southeast Asia, a culturally vibrant region that has not always received international recognition for its art. The exhibitions shown here, always colourful, engaging and full of visual interest, make use of photography, film and computer animation more often than traditional artistic media. Artists present issues that relate not only to esea experience but also to the region's diaspora, such as cross-cultural encounters, migration and displacement. A communal project space hosts events that bring together artists with members of the public to break down barriers and foster creative thinking.

The organisation has come a long way since it first opened in 1989 in Manchester's Chinatown as the Chinese Arts Centre, exhibiting the work of second and third generation Chinese British artists. It made the move to the Northern Quarter in 1997, signalling a desire to attract a mainstream audience and an international remit to show contemporary art from China, Taiwan, Hong Kong and the Chinese diaspora. The centre relocated to the Smithfield building in 2003 with a newly designed gallery that won an RIBA award for its architects, OMI of Manchester. Their scheme stylishly combines old and new. The original shop fronts have been retained, but with an eye-catching black metal entrance grille decorated with Chinese characters. In addition to spaces for exhibitions and events, there is a small shop full of intriguing gifts and books.

The gallery, renamed in 2013 the Centre for Chinese Contemporary Art, closed in 2021 but was relaunched in 2023 as esea contemporary with a new identity and a wider geographical focus unique in the UK. The organisation, an independent charity, benefits from Arts Council and local authority funding.

Address Market Buildings, 13 Thomas Street, Manchester M14 1EU, +44 (0)161 832 7271, www.eseacontemporary.org, hello@eseacontemporary.org | **Getting there** Tram (most lines) to Shudehill and 3-minute walk | **Hours** Tue–Sat 10am–5pm, Sun noon–5pm | **Tip** At the top of Shudehill, you can see the unusually shaped headquarters of the Co-operative Group, One Angel Square, a carbon-free building that has won numerous awards for sustainability.

38 __ FAC 251
Where Factory Records ended its days

The ground-breaking music label, Factory Records, was founded in 1978 by Alan Erasmus and Tony Wilson in Erasmus' house. In May of that year, the Factory name was used for a music club featuring the Durutti Column and Joy Division, but Factory Records only became the cultural focus of the Madchester post-punk music scene after their opening of the Haçienda in May 1982. Eight years later, flushed with success, Wilson and Erasmus moved the business into a former engineering works on the corner of Princess Street and Charles Street, which they named FAC 251. On the day it opened, the building was covered from top to bottom with posters for the Happy Mondays' new album *Bummed*. It was also here that the famous glass table that featured in the film *24 Hour Party People* was installed, suspended from the ceiling, at a cost of £80,000. The company's occupation of FAC 251, however, was brief, for in November 1992 it declared bankruptcy after a number of botched enterprises.

Following a period of vacancy, the building then became the city's premier gay club, Paradise Factory, before being remodelled and renamed FAC 251 once again for New Order's Peter Hook, whose book *The Haçienda – How Not to Run a Club* had just been released. Hook's designer was Ben Kelly, who had created the stylish interior of the Haçienda. The club has three levels, allowing for different music types and dance floors on any given evening. But why the name FAC 251? Because Wilson and Erasmus were obsessed with cataloguing. Everything that Factory Records produced had a FAC number: the company's anvil logo was FAC 47, an unfinished egg timer design was FAC 8, and even a lawsuit was FAC 61. The Haçienda was FAC 51 and the head office FAC 251. Generally known as the Factory, the present club draws on the legacy of the past but maintains the same ethos: promoting new bands and having a good time.

Address 112–118 Princess Street, Manchester M1 7EN, +44 (0)161 637 2570, www.factorymanchester.com | **Getting there** Tram (most lines) or train to Piccadilly and 10-minute walk | **Hours** Mon–Sat 11pm–4am | **Tip** If walking from Piccadilly Station to FAC 251, look out for the former Police and Fire Station on London Road, an Edwardian municipal showpiece that is being restored after long neglect.

39 Fairfield Moravian Settlement
Village of vision

A group of Moravian religious reformers came to Britain in 1730 *en route* for America. Some stayed and joined forces with local people who were opposed to the Church of England, the most ambitious project being Fairfield on the edge of Droylsden in the 1780s. It is an oasis of tranquillity in an otherwise unremarkable area. The Moravians aimed to be self-sufficient, its members engaged in farming, weaving, hat making and baking. The founders were John Lees, a local mine owner, and Benjamin Latrobe, whose son – also Benjamin – emigrated to America, became an architect and designed Washington's Capitol and the porticos of the White House. Before he left England, he had planned the Fairfield Settlement, with its cobbled squares and terraces of Georgian houses around a church. The buildings on each side of the church, now the school and community centre, were originally the Brethren's House and the Sisters' House, for single men and women, but the former was never a success as the men too readily succumbed to the temptations of drink and unruly behaviour. Part of the Sisters' House is now the museum, which records the life of the community, together with a display of everyday objects including pots and pans from the kitchens, grindstones and mallets from the workshop, gardening implements and a harmonium. One room is fitted out as a three-bed dormitory with simple patchwork quilts made by the Sisters.

Moravians emphasise fellowship and humanity. Love, they believe, should be the source of all actions. In times of hardship, they collected money for poor and invalid members of the community. The settlement ran counter to the exploitation of labour that underpinned the Industrial Revolution, and as a model of sustainability and cooperation, it is still relevant to our own times.

Address Fairfield Road, Droylsden M43 6AE, +44 (0)161 370 5199 | Getting there Tram to Droyslden (blue line) and 10-minute walk along Fairfield Road | Hours Museum open May–Aug Sat 1–4pm | Tip A group of attractive cottages built in 1914 on land owned by the Moravians, and designed by the Arts and Crafts architects Edgar Wood and Henry Sellers, can be found on Broadway, reached via a footpath alongside the burial ground.

40 Fireground
Fighting the flames

When Rochdale's Maclure Street fire station opened in 1933 it was the most up-to-date building of its kind in the country. At the flick of a switch all the electric lights and alarm bells would be activated throughout the station and the nearby firemen's houses, the front doors would open automatically, and a timer would start recording the speed of response. Over the next 90 years its firefighters tackled blazing warehouses, mills and homes, people trapped in burning vehicles and the wartime blitz. In 2014 the fire station closed, but with the help of retired service members it has reopened as a museum celebrating the world of fire safety and rescue across the Greater Manchester area.

On entering, the first sight is of a row of sparkling red and chrome fire engines spanning a period of 250 years. There are horse-drawn carriages and hand-operated pumps – one named Victoria and another George V. The biggest beast is a Dennis Big 6 Pump Escape dating from 1940 which is still in full working order. A street scene with houses damaged by the blitz is brought to life with light and sound effects, and there are films of fires and rescues showing the bravery of the fire crews. The Manchester region led the way in manufacture of fire appliances and on show are hoses and sprinklers, ladders and helmets (brass for the firemen and silver for the chief officer). The fireman's axe, stout boots and protective jackets are other vital items. Horses and dogs were once essential members of the team. The dogs would run ahead to clear the way for the horse-drawn engines: Rochdale's dog Nell led the crew barking a warning, and once saved the life of a child from under the path of a fast-moving engine. If you want to hear the stories there are brilliant volunteer ex-servicemen on hand. Meanwhile the kids will be happy dressing up as fire fighters and sliding down the pole ready for action.

Address Maclure Road, Rochdale OL11 1DN, +44 (0)1706 341219 | **Getting there** Tram (pink line) or train to Rochdale Railway Station | **Hours** Thu–Sat 10am–4pm | **Tip** Opposite is the Roman Catholic Church of St John the Baptist, built in the 1920s and modelled on Istanbul's Hagia Sofia, with fine mosaic murals inside. The fire station's hose drying tower makes up for the lack of a bell tower when seen from a distance.

41_Form Lifestyle Store
Small but perfectly formed

Elly Amoroso and Harry Williams, the proprietors of this small backstreet design shop, have a background in graphic design and retail, and believe in slow living, choosing to buy fewer, well-considered items that will serve their purpose and be appreciated for years to come. They have a keen eye for quality craft-made objects, favouring simplicity, functionality and care for the environment. Their stock comes directly from independents whose details appear on their website, and there are regular workshops at the store involving some of the makers.

Their pottery includes hand-thrown tableware by Sophie Fletcher of Zosia Ceramics, Cambridge, inspired by visits to Kettle's Yard. There is beautiful glassware ethically made from recycled glass in Bolivia, and blue and white tablecloths and bedspreads by the Women Weavers Association in Tanzania. Celebration candles made by Five Bees Yard in their Hertfordshire apiary are a welcome alternative to the usual candles found on birthday cakes. There is a nod to the Scandinavian look in the graphics and a wave to Japan in the meditative aroma products. Most items would serve as useful gifts, while the minimalist-style greetings cards would make anyone calm and happy.

The building is of interest too. This is one of a trio of two-room cottages, one up one down, added in the 1780s to the back of the more imposing houses on Lever Street erected 10 years earlier. Census returns record as many as 12 people living in this tiny cottage, showing how the once fashionable residential suburb was transformed into an area of textile workers. It has recently been cleverly restored with a glass-roofed atrium and spiral staircase. Tastefully equipped with predominantly beige or olive green objects, and devoid of clutter, the shop promotes a spartan lifestyle very different from that of the occupants it once housed.

Address 6 Bradley Street, Manchester M1 1EH, www.form-shop.com | **Getting there** 5-minute walk from Piccadilly Gardens | **Hours** Tue–Fri 11am–5.30pm, Sat 10.30–5pm, Sun 11am–4pm | **Tip** Another group of early dwellings can be found at 1–5 Kelvin Street dating from the 1770s. They were weavers' houses with long horizontal windows on the top floor to light the loom shops.

42 Frank Sidebottom
The man with the papier-mâché head

Chris Sievey, the comic genius behind Mancunian legend Frank Sidebottom, died penniless in 2010 at the age of 54. Sievey was spared a pauper's funeral by a crowdfunding campaign started by his friends, and three years later he was immortalised in a life-size bronze statue of his alter ego in his home town of Timperley. In 2018 *Being Frank*, a hilarious film about his insanely comic but also tragic life, starring Michael Fassbender, was released to wide acclaim.

Sievey's ambition was to be a pop star, but when his biggest hit, 'I'm in Love with the Girl on the Manchester Virgin Megastore Checkout Desk' reached number 54, his opportunity to appear on *Top of the Pops* was scuppered by a technicians' strike, and the record sank without trace. So, after years struggling to make it with his band, The Freshies, he changed direction and turned himself into a small man with a huge papier-mâché head singing versions of well-known songs in a nasal Manchester voice (behind the mask he had a swimming clip pegged to his nose), accompanied by a ukulele and his Oh Blimey Big Band.

At first, Frank was supposed to be the support act for The Freshies and their number-one fan, but soon people liked the support act more than the band, and the persona stuck. Frank played the part of a no-hoper, convinced he was on his way to the big time; it was a satire on the competitive world of show business that Sievey loved but failed to conquer and although it brought him a cult following, behind the mask his success was bitter-sweet.

The surreal humour is a prescient commentary on our present world where people can attain instant stardom for doing almost nothing. His death from cancer came suddenly and tragically, but the posthumous affection he received as a result of the film would have suited his sense of the absurd – fame arrived, but only after he had gone.

Address 363 Stockport Road, Timperley WA15 7UQ | **Getting there** Tram to Timperley (green line) and 15-minute walk | **Hours** Accessible 24 hours | **Tip** Boppin, a Madchester dance craze, was invented in Timperley by John Squire and Ian Brown, of the Stone Roses. They both grew up in Timperley and were often seen boppin down the road on their way to Altrincham Grammar School, in Marlborough Road, Bowdon.

43 Free Trade Hall
Where the Madchester sound took root

The Free Trade Hall is renowned as the concert hall where Bob Dylan was heckled with the chilling cry 'Judas' when he swapped his acoustic guitar for an electric one. For Manchester's younger generation of musicians, the Sex Pistols' gig there on 4 June, 1976 was even more life-changing. The provocative punk band was playing in the Lesser Free Trade Hall, a sweaty basement room with a capacity of 150, but such is the mythology that if all who claimed 'I was there' were assembled it would have been over 1,000. In fact, it was probably more like 50, but the effect it had on them was mind-blowing. The organisers were two students from Bolton Technical College, Howard Trafford and Pete McNeish who had just formed The Buzzcocks (after a week they changed their names to Howard Devoto and Pete Shelley). Six months later they issued their first vinyl, *Spiral Scratch*, which marked the creation of indie music. Pete Hook, a clerk at Salford Council was so impressed he went out next day and bought a bass guitar from Mazels on London Road. With his mate Bernard Sumner he went on to form Joy Division. Morrisey was inspired to write a letter to the *NME* about the Sex Pistols' concert in typically mocking terms 'Despite their discordant music and barely audible audacious lyrics, they were called back for two encores' – he thought he could do better.

Six weeks later the Sex Pistols returned for a second gig and this time, after all the hype, Tony Wilson and Martin Hannett, joint founders of Factory Records were seen, along with Mick Hucknall of Frantic Elevators and later Simply Red, Mark E. Smith who formed The Fall and went on to push the boundaries of punk, and of course the legendary Ian Curtis. It was a moment in musical history, not so much for the Sex Pistols' performance, but for the effect on those who were there. In Manchester, nothing would be the same again.

Address The Free Trade Hall is now a luxury hotel: The Edwardian Manchester, Peter Street, Manchester M2 5GP, +44 (0)161 835 9929, www.radissonhotels.com | Getting there Tram to St Peter's Square (all lines) | Tip The Oasis Club, a basement club at the top of nearby Lloyd Street, was the equivalent of Liverpool's Cavern Club. The Beatles played there in February 1962 but were upstaged by Manchester's own band The Hollies.

44 Gay Village
A proud history of queer culture

Manchester's LGBTQ+ scene has come a long way over the past 40 years. In the early 1980s, dark streets and closet bars were meeting places for gay men, and the shadowy and neglected Canal Street area was the favoured place to go. Club raids by the police were commonplace, and many suffered the public shame that led Alan Turing to take his life in 1954.

Today, that has all changed, and you are more likely to see the police being cheered on at the annual Pride parade through the city's streets. The opening of Manto in Canal Street in 1990 led to a new type of bar, its fully glazed frontage proclaiming 'out and proud', with drinkers spilling onto the street looking fabulous. Another game changer was the official recognition by the council of the Gay Village, later mischievously celebrated in the TV series *Queer as Folk* by Russell T. Davies.

In 1991, the first Manchester Pride parade 'The Carnival of Fun' was held, and over the years it has grown in strength. Today, it attracts thousands to the Gay Village over the August bank holiday weekend and includes a 'Pride Fringe' with arts, music and cultural events across the city, which is decked out in rainbow colours. The vast parade includes the army, police, NHS, city businesses and universities, football supporters and sports clubs among its floats, and raises thousands of pounds for LGBTQ+ causes. As the village has developed, however, tensions have emerged. Is it becoming too much of a focus for hen parties and friends out for a boozy weekend, or is it the stereotypical gay ghetto? Opinions are divided. There is no doubt that commercialism has altered the area's identity, just as attitudes to equality have changed; perhaps the need for specific gay districts may decline over time. But that is for the future; meanwhile, the Gay Village is still the place to be and be seen – 'we're here, we're queer, get used to it!'

Address Canal Street, Manchester M1 3HE | **Getting there** Free bus (route 1) to Princess Street or (route 2) to Chorlton Street | **Tip** Since the days of legendary Foo Foo Lamar, Manchester has been renowned for its drag queens, and Cruz 101 at 101 Princess Street, which was owned by Foo Foo in the 1990s, continues the tradition.

45 George Best's Mini
Booze, birds and fast cars

The first thing you see in the National Football Museum is George Best's black Mini Cooper, registration number G18 EST. It was his favourite car. He bought it in 2002, named it Susie after one of his cleaners and drove it until he was banned for drink-driving in 2004. Also at the museum is his school report from Grosvenor High School, East Belfast, where the youngster was rebuked for making 'no effort' in French and described merely as 'good' in physical education. The school specialised in rugby, so after playing truant he was moved to a football-playing school where he thrived.

'I think I've found you a genius,' a Manchester United talent scout reported back to Matt Busby after seeing the 15-year-old play. A master of the dribble, Best made his 1st Division debut in 1963 at the tender age of 17 and became a superstar when he scored two goals in a European Cup quarter-final match against Benfica, earning the nickname *O Quinto Beatle*. He capped this with the European Player of the Year Award 1968, but after that his career followed a downward slope. He took to partying, opening nightclubs and getting involved in brawls, and ended up playing his final game for the club in 1974.

Alcoholism was Best's downfall. He spent three months in prison in 1984 for drink-driving, assaulting a policeman and failing to observe bail. He continued to drink even after a liver transplant in 2002, and his death came three years later. There were tributes from the world's greatest players: Pelé, Diego Maradona and Johan Cruyff. Today, he is remembered for his brilliance on the pitch, and his witticisms off it. On the subject of enjoying the best of both worlds he remarked 'If you'd given me the choice of going out and beating four men and smashing a goal in from 30 yards against Liverpool or going to bed with Miss World, it would have been a difficult choice. Luckily, I had both.'

Address National Football Museum, Cathedral Gardens, Manchester M4 3BG, +44 (0)161 605 8200, www.nationalfootballmuseum.com | **Getting there** Tram (most lines) or train to Victoria | **Hours** Daily 10am–5pm | **Tip** The Old Nags Head, 19 Jackson's Row, M2 5WD is a shrine to George Best, and also features a roof garden mural by Stephen Lynn depicting Manchester celebrities; open daily 11am–11pm.

46 The Glade of Light
Memorial to the Arena Bombing

On May 22nd, 2017, an Islamist terrorist detonated a homemade bomb as people were leaving the Manchester Arena after attending a concert by the American singer Ariana Grande. 22 people were killed and over 1,000 were injured, many of them children. The incident caused shock and collective grief across the city, witnessed in the gathering of thousands at a vigil in Albert Square the following evening, and with floral tributes occupying St Ann's Square for months. Two weeks later Ariana Grande returned to Manchester to host a benefit concert *One Love Manchester* at Old Trafford Cricket Ground that was relayed on TV, radio and social media. This and an associated Red Cross appeal raised £17 million for victims of the attack and their families.

On the fifth anniversary, following an inquest into the atrocity and the jailing of the suicide bomber's brother for assisting in the crime, a memorial to the victims was opened by the Duke and Duchess of Cambridge. Titled *The Glade of Light*, at its centre is a 'halo' of white marble, with the names of those who lost their lives engraved in bronze. Memories and mementoes of them, provided by their loved ones, are contained in capsules embedded in the marble. Around the halo are trees and low-growing plants, creating a tranquil space for remembrance and reflection. It is located between Chetham's School of Music and the Cathedral in what is part of the city's medieval quarter, close to the Arena entrance. This has been transformed by pedestrianising Victoria Street, the once busy road that follows the River Irwell separating Manchester and Salford. The memorial garden is the first of a series of green spaces and walkways from Victoria Bridge to Victoria Station. In this peaceful and historic setting, the memorial makes a moving tribute to those who suffered and is a reminder that love is stronger than hate.

Address Victoria Street, Manchester M1 3SX | **Getting there** Tram (most lines) or train to Victoria and 5-minute walk | **Tip** On the corner of Victoria Bridge Road and Deansgate is La Vie Café serving a tempting range of savoury dishes, cakes and ice creams along with excellent coffee daily from 9am to 11pm.

47 Hallé St Peter's
Bringing music to the people

There used to be 11 churches and chapels in Ancoats and now there is only one, the Victorian church of St Peter. By the 1990s, the once densely populated area had become a ghost town, and the church was a ruin. Funds from the National Lottery and other bodies were raised to make it watertight, but only when the Hallé moved in and completed the restoration was the future of the church secured.

The world-renowned Hallé Orchestra has been a glorious presence in Manchester since 1857 when German immigrant Charles Hallé formed a band to play during the Art Treasures Exhibition. His band became a permanent orchestra for Manchester, synonymous with the Free Trade Hall, its home until 1996, when it moved to the new Bridgewater Hall. By this time, it was no longer enough for even the most famous orchestras to sit in a concert hall, perform and make recordings. Orchestras today go out into the community, building new audiences by working with schools and local groups, fostering young musicians and enabling people from all backgrounds to discover the joy of music.

From 2013, the orchestra began to use St Peter's for rehearsals, recordings and occasional small-scale performances, but in 2019 the Hallé was able to step up its activities in Ancoats when it opened the Oglesby Centre, a striking new building linked to the church. Designed by Manchester architects Stephenson Studio, it fronts onto Cutting Room Square with a bold modern façade in fashionably rusted Corten steel and hand-made linear bricks. Inside is the Victoria Wood Hall, a new home for the Children's Choir, of which she was a patron; a much-needed community and education room; Café Cotton which is open seven days a week. The main auditorium in the church has also been upgraded and it is a pleasure to attend a recital or an open rehearsal in this beautiful but informal setting.

Address 40 Blossom Street, Ancoats, M4 6BF, +44 (0)161 907 9000, https://halle.co.uk/venues/halle-st-peters | **Getting there** Bus 76, 83, 181 182 from Piccadilly Gardens to Oldham Road/New Cross | **Tip** From the corner of Oldham Street and Great Ancoats Street you can see an impressive mural depicting a despairing man resting his head on a bar. By the German artist Case, it was inspired by mental health issues.

48 Hanging Ditch
An ancient bridge revealed

In the Middle Ages a ditch separated the town of Manchester from the parish church (now the cathedral). It is thought that the ditch was part of a defensive system, possibly of Roman origin. The ditch connected the Rivers Irk and Irwell and was crossed by a bridge, first recorded in 1343 as Hengand Brigge, but rebuilt around 100 years later. As well as linking town and church, the bridge provided a shortcut across the churchyard for livestock being driven to the market place nearby.

Gradually the ditch was filled up with rubbish, until it became a nuisance and was culverted – in 1561 the local court issued an edict that no one was to throw 'any Donge fylthe or mucke upon or over the hanging bridge' – and the land was built up with houses. Long forgotten, the bridge was rediscovered below street level in the 1880s when demolition work was carried out and the site was opened to the public for three months. During this time, 32,000 people paid to view it, before it was concealed inside Hanging Bridge Chambers, the building that stands on the site. A century later it was revealed once more and restored as part of a new Cathedral Visitor Centre.

During excavation, the 'Donge' and 'mucke' was well sifted, revealing objects such as medieval shoes, pottery and animal bones that cast light on the history of the ditch. Being buried underground has preserved the bridge in good condition. It has two sandstone arches with a central pier, each differing in width and construction. One arch of the bridge can be seen from the paved area outside Hanging Bridge Chambers. Unfortunately the visitor centre has been closed, but by special arrangement with the Cathedral it is possible to gain access to the basement to make a closer inspection of what is one of Manchester's most ancient and intriguing structures.

Address 10 Cateaton Street, Manchester M3 1SQ, +44 (0)161 817 4817, www.manchestercathedralvisitorcentre.org | **Getting there** 5-minute walk | **Hours** Mon–Sat 10am–4pm | **Tip** The arched brick embankment with cobbled roadway crossing the river opposite the Hanging Ditch led up to Exchange Station. The station closed in 1969 and its site is now occupied by two monumental glass buildings.

49 Hat Works
Historical headgear

Hat Works is a quirky museum of the hat industry. Hats? You thought they came from Luton. Straw hats were made in Luton, felt hats were made in Stockport, and not only Stockport but Denton and Failsworth and the whole area in between. Hatting took over from cotton manufacture as the major industry of this area in the 1880s and lasted until the 1950s, but during the 1960s people stopped wearing hats and the industry went into steep decline. Now it has all but vanished, although there are still two flourishing hat companies, one in Denton and the other in Failsworth.

The museum is in Wellington Mill, Stockport, built originally as a cotton factory, but in 1895 it was taken over by Ward Brothers, specialists in hat finishing and trimming, and makers of a wide range of hats and caps. The bottom floor of the museum is about hat making, and explains the steamy, noisy and smelly industrial processes of making felt, and the shaping and moulding of the felt on blocks. There is also a block maker's workshop and machinery salvaged from local factories.

On the floor above is an entertaining display of hats of every imaginable kind – and some you couldn't dream up: the contemporary hats include a cauliflower fascinator and a patisserie hat that looks like a delicious fruit meringue adorned with raspberries and blackberries. (Did someone say 'I'll eat my hat'?) There are celebrity hats – one worn by Judi Dench, another by Fred Dibnah – a vast Royal Ascot hat by David Shilling, and historical hats – military helmets, stovepipe hats, bowlers and toppers, and 1950s trilbys and pork pie hats. In the section on faith hats you can see a Rastafarian cap and a Jewish yarmulke and learn the difference between a Muslim hijab (headscarf) and a niquab (veil). There are sporting hats – swimming, cricket and jockey caps – and tweed caps for country wear. Guess what you can buy in the gift shop?

Address Wellington Road South, Stockport SK3 0EU, +44 (0)161 474 2399, www.stockport.gov.uk/topic/hat-works, bookings.hatworks@stockport.gov.uk | **Getting there** Train to Stockport and 4-minute walk | **Hours** Thu–Sat 10am–4pm | **Tip** Robinson's Unicorn Brewery in Lower Hillgate still uses shire horses and you can meet them on tours of the brewery – book online via www.robinsonsbrewery.com.

50 Haweswater Aqueduct Mural
A neglected Manchester sculptor

Turn on the tap and water comes out. It's something we take for granted. Manchester's water supply comes from the Lake District, and heroic feats of engineering were required to get it here. A 96-mile aqueduct from Thirlmere was built between 1890 to 1925 and when more water was needed for the ever-growing city, a second aqueduct from Haweswater was started in 1935. It took 20 years to construct – 82 miles of underground tunnels carrying 570 million litres of water per day to a new reservoir in Heaton Park. A pumping station was built on the edge of the reservoir. On the side facing the street is a striking work of art commemorating the opening of the pipeline in 1955. It shows the pipeline coming forward from a stylised depiction of mountains and bending sharply round a corner; it passes three construction workers manhandling hydraulic machinery and ends in a funnel from which water gushes out. The relief, carved from Westmoreland greenstone, is the work of a now almost forgotten artist, Mitzi Cunliffe. Her combination of comic-strip simplicity with the clarity of a technical diagram was ahead of its time.

In the Manchester of the 1950s she was a prominent glamorous figure – a New Yorker, married to Marcus Cunliffe, an academic at Manchester University. She designed textiles, ceramics, glass and jewellery, but was best known for her large works: there are several in the Manchester area including fibreglass relief panels at the base of Owens Park tower, examples of the mass-produced architectural decorations that she called 'Sculpture by the Yard'. The Cunliffes lived at 18 Cranmer Road, Didsbury, where she converted the garage into her studio, now marked by a plaque. It was here that she created the one piece that everyone will recognise – the striking gold mask handed out to stars of film and TV at the annual BAFTA awards.

Address Heywood Road, Polefield, Prestwich M25 2RA | Getting there Bus 135 to Heywood Road and 10-minute walk | Hours Accessible 24 hours | Tip Take a ride through the park on a historic tram between the Lakeside Café and the park entrance on Middleton Road – operating Sat June–Sept noon–4.30pm and Sun June–Oct noon–4.30pm.

51 Higher Ground
Casual dining, seasonal sharing

Jaded foodies may pronounce that sharing plates are so last year, but at Higher Ground they are still very much alive, vibrant with flavour from locally grown produce, whole-animal butchery, and fresh fish and seafood. Higher Ground is the creation of three friends, Richard Cossins at front-of-house, wine expert Daniel Craig Martin and Head Chef Joe Otway formerly of Where the Light Gets In (see ch. 108); they and their well-trained team are happy to chat about the dishes and advise on the wine list, which favours low-intervention makers from across Europe. The three have worked in leading fine-dining restaurants worldwide but there is nothing pretentious about their food: no freakish pairings, just delicious combinations such as heritage beetroot with gooseberry and herb mayo or house-smoked trout, crab and celeriac. Key to the daily-changing menu is Cinderwood Market Garden, Cheshire, set up by the trio: 'If you get locally sourced, well grown produce that hasn't been shipped for days and days and is picked in its peak ripeness, by hand, it tastes better and it makes it easier to translate that into dishes,' explains Joe. Offerings might also include tasty Knutsford Hogget (older than lamb, younger than mutton) or Garstang Blue cheese, but there are also quality ingredients from further afield: fresh oysters and a pillowy cheese tart made from Pitchfork Cheddar are signature favourites.

The spacious modern interior is bounded on two sides by floor to ceiling plate glass walls. Choose a table by the window or sit at the long counter, from where you can watch the chefs at work in the open kitchen right in front of you. They look relaxed, as if they are enjoying themselves, a mood which transfers itself to the diners. Why 'Higher Ground'? The restaurant started life in a cabin on stilts, at Kampus (see ch. 64). It may have descended to street level, but the food is still the tops.

Address Faulkner House, New York Street, Manchester M1 4DY, +44 (0)161 236 2931, highergroundmcr.co.uk, booking advisable | Getting there Tram (most lines) or bus to Piccadilly Gardens | Hours Lunch Thu 12.30–3.30pm, Fri & Sat 12.30–4pm, Dinner Wed & Thu 5–11pm, Fri & Sat 5.30pm–midnight | Tip The same team is responsible for Flawd, 9 Keeper's Quay, New Islington, a pocket-sized wine bar and bottle shop serving natural wines, craft beers, charcuterie and cheese.

52 — Holy Name of Jesus
Masterpiece by the designer of the hansom cab

The Church of the Holy Name, built in 1871 for the Jesuits, is grand enough to be a cathedral. It was designed by Joseph Aloysius Hansom, famous for the invention of the two-wheeled cab that bears his name; and along with Arundel Cathedral it is one of his two finest buildings. The style is 13th-century French Gothic, with flying buttresses and rose windows reminiscent of Amiens and Rheims. Hansom intended it to have a 73-metre-high tower and steeple, based on Amiens, but only the lower part was built; the octagonal top section was added in 1928 by Adrian Gilbert Scott. Shafts of light falling from the high windows penetrate the gloom of the spacious interior, while tiny candles flicker in the chapels. Only the slenderest of columns support the roof vaults, which are formed of hollow terracotta blocks instead of stone to reduce the weight. The ornamental wall facings are also terracotta. Superb furnishings include the high altar by Hansom's son Joseph Stanislaus, the ornate St Joseph chapel and the chapel of the Madonna delle Strade (Our Lady of the Streets) by J. F. Bentley, the architect of Westminster Cathedral.

Although the church has a medieval character, the Jesuits' main idea was to teach the faith by giving celebrants maximum visibility of the solemn Mass, together with preaching and ritual. But in 1985 they closed the church and left. A few years later a community of Oratorian priests boldly took it on and started a huge renovation project.

This work continues today under the Jesuits who returned to Manchester, taking over the university chaplaincy and moving back in. For Smiths fans, however, the church may be better known for the surreal image from the album *The Queen is Dead* where Morrisey was minding his own business lifting lead off the roof of the Holy Name church and spied the dancing 'Vicar in a Tutu'.

Address 339 Oxford Road, Manchester M13 9PG, +44 (0)161 273 1456, www.holyname.info | **Getting there** Bus 41, 42, 43, 142, 143 or 147 to Manchester University | **Hours** Mon–Sat 11am–1pm (Mass at 12.30pm), Sun 10am–noon & 6–8pm (Mass at 11am & 7pm) | **Tip** The actual Roman Catholic Cathedral is in Chapel Street, Salford, though it is not as magnificent as the Holy Name.

53 Imperial War Museum North

Deconstructivism at Salford Quays

Deconstructivism is the term used for buildings that give the impression of controlled chaos, often with fragmented outlines, walls set at crazy angles and sloping floors. One of the leading exponents of this architectural movement is Daniel Libeskind, whose most famous project is the Jewish Museum in Berlin, which consists of three curved elements that collide with one another, symbolising the destruction of war. His design for the Imperial War Museum North embodies similar ideas. Libeskind was born in Poland and had many relatives who were murdered in the Holocaust; he was also aware of those who suffered in the Manchester Blitz, which targeted Trafford Park and its engineering works. His concept for the Salford museum was a shattered globe, 'reassembled as a fundamental emblem of conflict.' The fragments take the form of shards, representing the war on land (the downward curving part), in the air (the tall upright part) and the war at sea (the up-curved part overlooking the Ship Canal). The internal spaces are disconcerting, mostly windowless, with jutting wall planes, zigzag ceiling lights and floors at different angles, inducing a feeling of disorientation, intensified by the frightening instruments of war on display.

Starchitects' buildings are renowned for running over budget, but the reverse happened here. Originally costed at £40 million, the museum was completed in 2001 for £28.5 million after the National Lottery failed to support it. The major funders were the EU (£8.9 million) and Peel Holdings, owner of the Manchester Ship Canal (£12.5 million), the latter said to be the largest sum ever given to a UK cultural project by a private company. In spite of the economies, the concept of the shattered globe survived to make the museum the most powerful work of architecture erected in the Manchester region in the last 100 years.

Address IWM North, The Quays, Trafford Wharf Road, Manchester M17 1TZ, www.iwm.org.uk | **Getting there** Tram to Imperial War Museum (red line) | **Hours** Daily 10am–5pm | **Tip** The Lowry Arts Centre by Michael Wilford & Partners (2000), visible across the footbridge, also has aspects of deconstructivism; although imposing in scale and ambition, it lacks the rigour and conviction of the War Museum.

54_Jandol
Lebanese delight

This brightly lit family-run café-restaurant on Stockport Road specialises in baklava, delicately crisp sweet filo pastry layered with chopped pistachios, cashews or walnuts, and cut into tiny squares and diamonds or rolled up into fingers. Most people first taste baklava on holiday in Greece, where it tends to be oozing with syrup, sickly-sweet, but Lebanese baklava are different – lighter and more subtle, sweet without being cloying. At Jandol, you can buy some to take away or sit at a table and enjoy them with a cup of cardamom or mint tea. If you don't know which of the many different kinds to try, the friendly Tania will make a selection for you, or you can buy an assortment beautifully presented on a gift tray and wrapped in shiny cellophane. Indeed, everything in the shop is super-glossy, from the chandeliers to the shelves of trinkets and gilded tea sets.

Jandol is packed with goodies: there are piles of nougat and marzipan studded with nuts, sugared almonds in all colours of the rainbow, jars of honey and trays of crystallised fruits. The pastries and sweets are freshly prepared to traditional Lebanese recipes handed down over the generations. Besides baklava, there are mahmoule, delectable little cakes made with semolina and stuffed with dates or nuts; Turkish delight in an assortment of flavours – pomegranate, orange, rose, cherry; and deliciously flaky halva, made from tahini and pistachios. Jandol also serves a full menu of authentic Lebanese food. The mezze are a good bet for lunch – hummus, baba ganoush, loubieh (beans stewed in tomato), vine leaves, kibbeh and falafel – and there are salads and meat dishes such as kebabs and shawarmas. Alex, the chef, is also expert at Western-style patisserie, coloured macarons and fruit tarts, but the lure of the East beckons. Why choose cream cakes when those glistening trays of baklava are waiting?

Address 861 Stockport Road, Levenshulme, Manchester M19 3PW, +44 (0)161 225 5502, www.jandolrestaurant.co.uk | **Getting there** Train to Levenshulme, or 192 bus to Albert Road, Levenshulme | **Hours** Sun–Thu 10am–11pm, Fri & Sat 9am–11pm | **Tip** Further down Stockport Road at no. 965 is Levenshulme Antiques Village in the former Levenshulme Town Hall, worth a look for the Victorian interiors as well as for the eclectic array of antiques.

55 John Rylands Library Entrance Hall
Valhalla of the book

Be sure not to miss the most spectacular part of John Rylands Library, the old entrance hall. Today, visitors go in through a new wing with a lift for disabled access, but this means the original entrance hall doesn't really have a function any more – apart from leading to the historic toilets, complete with wooden seats and old-fashioned pull chains (there are modern facilities in the new wing). The architect of the library, Basil Champneys, deserves to be better known, for in the old entrance hall and staircase he provided a staggering display of architectural fireworks: impossibly slender columns support soaring stone vaulting, the vertiginous staircase sweeps round and upwards with an eye-popping circular balcony high above, and everywhere light bulbs sprout like exotic blooms from bronze fittings with flowing Art Nouveau detailing. After all this, the reading room comes as a contrast, calm and majestic, like a cathedral.

The library, which opened in 1900, was founded by the formidable Mrs Enriqueta Rylands, the daughter of a Cuban sugar grower. She came to Manchester as the companion of the first wife of cotton millionaire John Rylands and ended up by marrying him: he was 74, she was 32. After he died, she spent his fortune on building the library and buying books for it.

It was originally intended to specialise in bibles and theological literature but Mrs Rylands astutely purchased two outstanding collections of rare books formed by British aristocrats Lord Spencer and Lord Crawford, and ever since, the library has acquired precious books, manuscripts and archives of all kinds. The library was one of the first buildings in Manchester to be lit by electricity and had an early form of air-conditioning to keep out the foul Manchester air.

Address 150 Deansgate, Manchester M3 3EH, +44 (0)161 306 0555, www.library.manchester.ac.uk/rylands | Getting there 7-minute walk from St. Peter's Square | Hours Wed – Sat 10am – 5pm | Tip In nearby Lincoln Square is a gigantic statue of Abraham Lincoln, commemorating the support of Manchester cotton workers for the Union states during the American Civil War.

56 — Karl Marx's Desk
The oldest public library in Britain

Chetham's Library was founded in the mid-17th century by Humphrey Chetham, a wealthy cloth merchant, but the building that houses the library, originally a college for priests, is older still, dating back to 1421. It is the oldest building in the city centre and probably the most atmospheric. Go through the Gothic entrance arch into the picturesque courtyard and you are in another world, sealed off from modern Manchester. A small doorway at the far end leads through smoke-blackened stone corridors and upstairs to the library, a series of long narrow spaces lined with tall bookcases secured behind wooden gates. Beyond is the grand wood-panelled reading room, with a portrait of Chetham and a florid display of his coat of arms between twin obelisks standing on books, depicted in carved and painted wood.

The library is full of treasures – manuscripts, diaries, letters and rare books – and is especially rich in archives about the social and economic history of the North West. Many well-known people came here to study, including Daniel Defoe and Benjamin Franklin, but the most influential visitors were two young Germans who came in the early years of Queen Victoria's reign.

At one side of the reading room is a little Gothic alcove with a small table. It was here that Karl Marx and his friend Friedrich Engels sat in the summer of 1845 and over a period of 6 weeks read 13 volumes about British society and political economy, filling three exercise books with detailed notes. If you visit the library today, you can actually sit at the table and read replica copies, beautifully made with leather bindings, of the same books. For Marx, this was the first of many visits to Manchester, but Engels had already been there for some time: their studies and their experience of social conditions in the city were vital to the development of their world-changing political writings.

Address Long Millgate, Manchester M3 1SB, +44 (0)161 834 7961, www.chethams.org.uk | **Getting there** Tram (most lines) or train to Victoria | **Hours** Readers by appointment only, Mon–Fri 9am–12.30pm & 1.30–4.30pm; tours Mon–Fri, check website for times, booking essential | **Tip** Adjoining the library is the Stoller Hall, a beautiful new music venue with outstanding acoustics. Although linked to Chetham's School of Music, its concerts and recitals are open to the public. It won a national RIBA award in 2017.

57 Kiku
Glamour in the Northern Quarter

Kiku, corsetière and lingerie boutique, wins the prize for the most original window displays in Manchester. A corset shop window? In the old days, you might see an unappetising creation for the fuller figure in creaky pink satin, maybe with a bit of lace (very daring), but this is something else: a surreal vision of striped corsets, floaty chiffon scarves and silk lounging pyjamas, wittily combined with carnival masks, long gloves, fans and fascinators. The windows change regularly with black lace and Gothic batwings for Halloween and decadent party dresses for Christmas – a free show that all tastes and genders will enjoy.

Kiku (Japanese for chrysanthemum) is the brainchild of Lyn McKay, who describes her shop as a gigantic dressing-up box. Although she sells off-the-peg garments such as a fabulous range of kimonos, the core of the business is made-to-measure. Bolts of fabric are piled up everywhere, with rolls of trimmings and unusual buttons.

If it's a corset you want, you can choose from a lavish selection of materials, new or vintage, embellished with whatever you fancy – lace, embroidery, beads or ribbons. You can select the shape that suits your body type: the classic Kiku design is based on an 1890s hourglass silhouette, but Lyn is happy to create something different just for you.

She will also make bespoke lingerie and dresses whether it's a crinoline, a Hollywood-style strapless number for the red carpet, or a head-turning outfit for your non-white wedding. Stage wear is a speciality; burlesque performers are some of her best customers and cross-dressers are welcome. As for the hats, ready-to-wear or customised, the delightfully dotty range includes berets and pillboxes to wear perched at crazy angles, cloches and turbans, all adorned to taste with sequins, bows or bits and bobs on wobbly wires. Why would you ever go to Marks & Spencer again?

Address 100 Tib Street, Manchester M4 1LR, +44 (0)161 819 5031, www.kikuboutique.co.uk | **Getting there** Tram (most lines) or bus to Shudehill and 5-minute walk | **Hours** Mon–Fri 10.30am–6pm, Sat 10.30–5pm | **Tip** Also on Tib Street, at no. 58, is Northern Flower, a delightful potting-shed-style flower shop full of unusual plants and containers.

58 Kim's Kitchen
Brutalism meets kitsch

Formerly Kim-by-the-Sea, Kim's Kitchen may have changed its name, but it remains a joyful and friendly restaurant on an isolated street corner in Hulme. It occupies a small part of a flagship building that followed in the wake of a catastrophic upheaval of the local community. In the last 30 years of the 20th century, the Hulme Crescents, 'one of the most notoriously defective and dysfunctional housing estates in Europe,' replaced the old terraces. When the Crescents were in turn demolished, the social fabric of the area fell apart. An activist group came together to create a vibrant cultural scene influenced by the collectivist Freetown Christiania in Denmark, and in 1999 the locals formed a cooperative called Homes for Change. With support from the council they colonised the strange new building, a mix of apartments and workspaces with Kim's Kitchen acting as a hub for members and the community.

    The kitchen serves old favourites such as Bob's Bajun Curry Goat, Beer Battered Cod and Wings of the Week, with specials such as Uncle John's Cheese and Onion Pie, Greek Salad or Bangers and Mash. Just what your Mum would make. Breakfast and lunch is served until 4pm: you can have the English full works or the healthy Med option of hummus, falafel and roasted veg. Portions are generous and fantastic value. At the bar are offbeat cocktails, wines, continental beers and a long list of rums. Above all it's the eclectic internal décor you will remember, a mixture of concrete ceilings with an upside-down view of the Hulme Crescents (which serve as soundproofing for the flats above), clashing colours and paintings by local artists. The mezzanine bar, furnished with mismatching leather sofas and comfy old cinema seats, has panels telling the heroic history of Hulme. On warm nights, enjoy the large beer garden, a chunk of concrete street left over from the years of tragic regeneration.

Address 49 Old Birley Street, Manchester M15 5RF, +44 (0)161 232 7667, www.kimbythesea.wixsite.com | **Getting there** Bus 86 to Royce Street, Hulme and 5-minute walk | **Hours** Mon, Wed–Sat noon–11pm, Sun noon–10pm (closed Tue) | **Tip** Across the road is the lively Hulme Community Garden Centre promoting sustainability, urban gardening, civic engagement, food production, independent living, health and well-being.

59 Kimpton Clock Tower Hotel

Tiles by the mile

Built as the headquarters of the mighty Refuge Assurance Company, the Kimpton Clock Tower Hotel is one the most spectacular buildings in Manchester. The Refuge was established in 1858 as a friendly society helping the poor of Dukenfield on the eastern edge of Manchester; it grew quickly to become one the country's greatest life insurance and pension providers. In 1890 Alfred Waterhouse, famous for Manchester Town Hall and the Natural History Museum, London, was engaged to design the company's new offices on this corner site. Clad in hard red brick and terracotta, the building was made to withstand the soot and smog of the city. After Alfred's death, his son Paul was called in to double it in size, adding the soaring clock tower and new entrance on Oxford Road in 1912. A further large extension on Whitworth Street followed in the 1930s.

The interiors surpass the exterior for splendour, with walls of glittering Burmantofts tiles in shades of cream and brown, richly coloured stained glass and decorative wrought iron. The corner entrance lobby that now leads to the bar and restaurant is especially lavish, while the main entrance rotunda that accommodated the chairman's automobile has become a stylish hotel foyer. The bar, a calm space by day, buzzes with life in the evening and has DJs at the weekend. Drinks can also be taken in the Winter Garden Conservatory or the 'Den' for those addicted to table football and snooker. Other attractions are the marble and bronze full-height staircase and the largest ballroom in the north of England. Statuettes of Industry and Thrift, symbolising the ethical principles of the Refuge, flank the entrance gates to this opulent palace of consumption: such were the foundations on which the wealth of Manchester was built.

Address Oxford Street, Manchester M60 7HA, +44 (0)161 288 1111, www.kimptonclocktowerhotel.com | Getting there Train to Oxford Road or free bus (route 1) to Whitworth Street/Palace Theatre | Tip More large-scale terracotta-clad buildings front Whitworth Street, which was created in the boom that followed the opening of the Manchester Ship Canal in 1894. Pre-eminent are Lancaster House, Bridgewater House and India House, with its elegantly arched ironwork gate.

60 LANX
Choose Lancashire shoes

If you want proper shoes, handmade, built to last and fashionable, LANX is the shop for you. Back in 2016, Lancashire-born Marco Vaghetti abandoned a marketing career and went on a six-month, 10-country tour to learn all he could about shoemaking. Inspired by the Japanese and Chinese craftsmen he met on his journey and buoyed up by the shoemakers' secrets he gathered en route, he decided to set up LANX, a workshop in his home county to make shoes of the highest quality.

At first, Marv, as he is known, sold the shoes, mainly brogues, at markets across the north-west, meeting his customers and responding to their wishes. But since then, the company has grown steadily, with a highly skilled team of young shoemakers and an ever-expanding range of footwear for both men and women. The collection includes shoes and brogues, lace-up and elastic-sided boots, hiker boots and sneakers. All have been designed in-house, and the majority have been handmade in Britain, either at their workshop in Whalley, or at other family-run shoe factories. LANX supports local suppliers for the leather and other materials used in production but also seeks out small-scale European companies such as Vibram, whose Italian rubber compound soles are used in the LANX 365 all-purpose boots to give support and stability as well as a firm grip on icy surfaces.

The small corner shop in the Northern Quarter is lined with serried ranks of shoes and boots. The furnishings are restricted to a single large box for sitting on while you test the footwear for size. The robust display echoes the character of the Whalley premises, where there is a larger shop alongside the workshop. As for branding, a discreet Lancashire Rose and the White Bull motif they have adopted are tokens of quality. But should you fancy something more showy for your boots, a bespoke shoe tattooing service is on hand.

Address 7 Oak Street, Manchester M4 5JD, www.lanxshoes.com, hello@lanxshoes.com | **Getting there** Wed–Sat 10am–6pm, Sun noon–5pm | **Hours** Wed–Sat 10am–6pm, Sun noon–5pm | **Tip** Just Between Friends Coffee, around the corner at 56 Tib Street, is a similarly pocket-sized café serving intensely flavoured single-origin coffees, cakes and delicious toasted sandwiches.

61   Lark Hill Place
Remembrance of Salford past

In the 1950s, close-knit communities were being destroyed with the demolition of Victorian terraces and rehousing in overspill estates. For the curator of Salford Museum, this was an opportunity to collect not works of art, but old shop fronts, signs, food packets and ordinary items of the kind that most people throw away without a thought. Even the children attending the museum's Saturday Club were enlisted to search skips and ransack their grandparents' homes for bits and pieces to go in the museum. The resulting display is enchanting: a late Victorian cobbled street of shops and houses, with a carriage, penny-farthing bicycles and an old post box.

The shop windows are a delight: there is a toy shop with a rocking horse, a whip and top and a Noah's Ark; a general store with groceries and sweets – packets of Mintos and Victory lozenges; a dressmaker selling hats and lace; a clogger for mending boots and shoes; and a chemist's shop with rows of drug jars in mahogany cabinets, tins of pills and ointments and space for weighing and mixing medicines. It's always teatime here, the gas lamps have just been lit and through the window of a Victorian parlour you can catch a glimpse of a table laid for tea.

Some people might regard the whole thing as a bit phoney: the picturesque Blue Lion pub was made up of items from several local hostelries, and the dim lighting that adds so much to the atmosphere has a utilitarian purpose, as it protects the artefacts from fading. There are lessons in class difference with a glimpse into an artisan's cottage contrasting with the middle-class Victorian parlour and a fancy drawing room in the Georgian house across the street, yet it is a rose-tinted view of a past where there were no slums and everyone could afford to eat. However, if nostalgia is not your thing, there is always the People's History Museum as an antidote.

Address Salford Museum and Art Gallery, Peel Park, The Crescent, Manchester M5 4WU, +44 (0)161 778 0800, www.salfordmuseum.com | **Getting there** Bus 35, 36 or 37 to Salford University or train to Salford Crescent | **Hours** Tue–Fri 9.30am–4pm, Sat & Sun 11.30–4pm | **Tip** Behind the museum is Peel Park, visited by Queen Victoria in 1851 – statues of her and Prince Albert are in front of the museum. The park has been carrying out improvements, funded by a National Lottery grant.

62 Legh Road, Knutsford
The Witches' Sabbath

The genteel Georgian town of Knutsford boasts the craziest group of villas in England. They were built by a wealthy glove maker, Richard Harding Watt, between 1902 and 1906, inspired by his extensive travels in Italy, the Middle East and Australia. Watt worked with a number of architects but made it abundantly clear what he wanted from them, issuing them with his own sketches and sacking them if he didn't like what they produced. He had a passion for towers with jagged outlines, domes, inscriptions and randomly placed windows, with touches of Japonaiserie and Art Nouveau as well as Italianate and Islamic features.

The eight outrageous houses he built on Legh Road are also scattered with architectural salvage from demolished buildings in Manchester, including classical columns, pediments, sills, floorboards and even reused doors. The largest house, Aldwarden Hill, has a Doric Lodge that originally stood in front of the Manchester Infirmary in Piccadilly; it was brought here and re-erected complete. The Round House, a little further along Legh Road, at first appears to be a joke since it is square, but hidden from the road is an attached round tower, and in the garden is a round summerhouse in the form of an upside-down cabbage.

What are we to make of these eccentric buildings? The architectural historian Nikolaus Pevsner wrote in 1971 that they were a 'monstrous desecration' and a 'Witches' Sabbath,' while Stephen Spielberg used Legh Road as a substitute for Shanghai in his classic film *Empire of the Sun*. When Watt was asked near the end of his life whether his inspiration came from Italy, he replied with great conviction that this was 'British architecture.' For him they were an all-consuming obsession, and indeed he died in 1913 after falling from his carriage while standing to admire their whimsical skyline from across the valley.

Address Legh Road, Knutsford WA16 8LP | **Getting there** Train to Knutsford and 10-minute walk | **Tip** Other Watt buildings can be found in the centre of Knutsford, including the Gaskell Memorial Tower and King's Coffee House, celebrating the novelist Elizabeth Gaskell, whose novel *Cranford* was based on life in the town.

63 Library Walk Link
A beautiful folly?

It seems strange that Manchester's Central Library and Town Hall Extension, the two imposing buildings that enclose the north side of St Peter's Square, were designed by the same architect – Vincent Harris – and built at much the same time – in the 1930s. For one is in the classical style, and pays homage to the Pantheon in Rome, while the other is neo-Gothic, in deference to Waterhouse's Town Hall. An elegantly curved open passageway, Library Walk, runs between the buildings emphasising their separate identities. When it was first announced, a proposal to erect a new foyer within Library Walk, linking the two buildings and closing the passageway at night, was strongly opposed.

The public protest, however, was overruled and now that the link is complete, how should we view the result? Faced with the challenge of joining two buildings of strikingly different character, the architects, SimpsonHaugh and Partners, bravely decided to insert a structure that bears no relation to either. Yet as a work of both architecture and sculpture, it makes its own bold statement. It is also technically advanced, using huge panels of curved glass to support the 30-tonne roof; the lack of any obvious structural supports meaning that it has a minimal impact on the visibility of the curved walkway. You can't miss the undulating mirror-polished stainless steel ceiling with its crazy reflections of passers-by, but look down at the floor too, for among the tiny Tudor rose mosaics, copies of those found in the Town Hall, are 18 incorporating people's names, illuminated from below by red lights. These record victims of the Peterloo Massacre.

So what is the verdict? Is the Library Walk Link a successful addition to the townscape or an extravagant folly? As with Brexit, opinion remains divided, but it is a pleasure to walk through and a quirky addition to Library Walk.

Address St Peter's Square, Manchester M2 5PD, +44 (0)161 236 1983 | **Getting there** Tram to St Peter's Square (most lines) | **Hours** Daily 8am–10pm | **Tip** From the Library Link, you can go into the Town Hall Extension and see the beautifully decorated Rates Hall, where Manchester citizens used to pay their rates. It has been magnificently restored, also by SimpsonHaugh.

64 Little David Street
A secret place revealed

A narrow cobbled street, chained off for years and filled with abandoned tyres, has been purposefully brought back to life. It runs between two historic warehouses on the edge of the Gay Village that have been converted into apartments as part of the wider Kampus development and leads to a beautifully landscaped garden. The garden was originally a wharf alongside the Rochdale Canal serving the two warehouses but was filled in long ago and used as a car park. The brick and stone cotton warehouses date from the mid-19th century; one was the premises of Minto and Turner, whose nameplate remains high on the gable wall. The other, Minshull House, became the manufacturing hub of fashion company Baracuta's classic G9 Harrington Jacket, worn by Elvis Presley and James Dean. Within the garden you will find items salvaged from the warehouses including a cast iron cotton packing press and a weighing machine from the 1860s, and in Little David Street is a New York-style escape staircase and a goods hoist both attached to the brick walls.

A range of food and drink independents surround the garden. With a first-floor balcony in the sun is the stylish wine bar Beeswing and below is Nell's New York Pizza and Bar. Pollen Bakery with its famed sourdough and Viennese patisserie is another good choice. Yum Cha provides a different note with dim sum and other Chinese delicacies. Madre and Salon Madre (a bar and pool hall) bring a taste of Mexican hospitality to Manchester with tacos, mezcal and tequila, plus films of Lucha Libre (Mexican wrestling) if you're in the mood. The Maker's Quarter has co-working studios for creatives alongside Kolab, which sells handmade products by local makers. The Kampus aim is to create a neighbourhood with its own special character in the heart of the city. With its relaxed ambience, attractive setting and great food and drink offers it should succeed. Just hope the rain keeps off.

Address Little David Street, Manchester M1 3FY | **Getting there** Free bus (routes 1 or 2) to Chorlton Street | **Hours** Accessible 24 hours | **Tip** Opposite the Kampus entrance on Minshull Street is the Crown Courts, an impressive neo-Gothic building of 1873 by Thomas Worthington. Note the fierce carved dragons clinging to the sides of the doorways that hint at the unknown terrors of judicial sentence.

65 Mackie Mayor
Cuisine from eight kitchens

Smithfield Market in the Northern Quarter was once the largest covered market complex in Britain but by the 1970s most of the buildings had closed. The Victorian meat market, announcing its function with a magnificent stone bull's head over the entrance, became in turn a training centre for unemployed youngsters, a shop-mobility centre and a skateboard park, but they all folded and the building was left empty for decades. It was spotted by Nick Johnson, formerly of Urban Splash, the developer that prides itself on regenerating properties that no one else dares touch. With his partner Jenny, he had already created a successful foodie venue at Altrincham Market House and he did it again in Manchester: communal dining at long tables in the centre of the hall served by independent kitchens plus beer, wine and cocktail bars.

It's a feast for the eyes – and nose – just to wander round to see what's cooking and watch the chefs at work whether they are doing breakfast, brunch or prepping for dinner. You choose whatever you fancy, not necessarily from the same counter, and the food is brought to your table. Johnson has chosen his vendors carefully with an emphasis on fresh, local and sustainable. Offerings include curries and stir-fries from Chilli B, tasty burgers and steaks from Tender Cow, and Honest Crust's wood-fired sourdough pizzas. For Japanese food fans, there's New Wave Ramen, while Eagle Street coffee serves ice-cream and donuts. The wine bar is run by Didsbury-based Reserve Wines while Jack in the Box beer bar sells craft beers from its own Blackjack Manchester brewery. The Mackie building has been restored with its rough brick walls exposed and a reclaimed wooden floor, giving the glass-roofed market hall a touch of contemporary industrial chic. Why the name? Ivie Mackie was Mayor of Manchester when the building first opened and his name is still over the entrance.

Address 1 Eagle Street, Manchester M4 5BU, www.mackiemayor.co.uk | **Getting there** Tram (most lines) or bus to Shudehill and 5-minute walk | **Hours** Tue–Sat 9am–10pm, Sun 9am–6pm | **Tip** The Wholesale Fish Market on Thomas Street has been half-demolished but the front wall is still standing, with decorative gates and sculptured reliefs showing the catching and selling of fish.

66 Man City Changing Room
The Soul of the Squad

The Manchester City Stadium tour starts in the exhibition area where the team's story is told from its inception. Like most football clubs, it's a tale of ups and downs. The first major period of success was in the late 1960s and '70s. Then, after years spent in the shadow of their rivals across town, City's greatness was recaptured with limitless cash from its Gulf owners and brilliant leadership from Pep Guardiola. The highlight was top UEFA European ranking in 2023, since when the winning touch has stalled. The tour ends with a 360° film looking to the future: hopefully one of better luck. Along the way, amiable guides lead you through the arrivals entrance, VIP stands, dug-out, hospitality suite, tunnel, and the climax – the home team changing room.

The stadium was built to host the 2002 Commonwealth Games and was adopted by Man City a year later. It has won many awards and has one of the best Premier League pitches. Improvements have followed, including the players' facilities. Tour members see the away team's changing room first, generous in scale and painted a calming shade of grey. But it is nothing compared to the home team's circular space, more than twice the size, with built-in lockers and named seats for each member of the squad. The manager arranges the seating plan, with no two players from the same nation next to one another. There is a warm-up room with state-of-the-art exercise machines, surrounded by full-size group photos of the squad to put them in a collaborative frame of mind. Hydrotherapy pools and ice baths are for use after the match. The tunnel, running through the centre of the hospitality suite, is lined in one-way mirror glass so the players can be seen, but don't see the VIPs when heading out for the kick-off. And 'after the match', a virtual Pep turns up in the press room for a Q&A and selfies with tour members – don't the fans just love him?

Address Etihad Campus, Manchester M11 3FF, +44(0) 161 444 1894 | **Getting there** Tram to Etihad Campus (blue line) and 5-minute walk | **Hours** Normally six tours a day, more restricted on match days, telephone for details | **Tip** The centrepiece of the nearby Beswick Community Hub is *Dad's Halo Effect*, a sculpture by Ryan Gander consisting of three giant stainless steel chess pieces in an ambiguous checkmate position.

67 — The Manchester Baby
Freddie's world-changing computer

The machine in the Manchester Science and Industry Museum looks like something out of the children's book *The Incredible Adventures of Professor Branestawm*. It's 5.2 metres long – an unwieldy assemblage of valves, dials and cathode ray tubes, connected by crazy loops of wiring and mounted on frames over 2 metres tall. In 1948 Freddie Williams, Professor of Electro-technics at the University of Manchester, was squinting at a lot of flickering dots on one of the tubes when suddenly the dots stopped moving. It was a eureka moment. He had proved that a computer could store not only the numbers, but also the instructions used to perform calculations. The Manchester Baby (official title: the Small-Scale Experimental Machine) was the world's first stored-program computer, the earliest working machine to contain all the elements essential to a modern electronic computer.

Williams knew about cathode ray tubes from his work on radar systems during World War II. He and his former pupil Tom Kilburn designed and built the Baby to test his discovery that the tubes could be used for electronic storage. On 21 June, 1948 they programmed the Baby with a complex mathematical problem. The machine, having performed around three and a half million operations, produced the correct answer. It took about 52 minutes: the Baby was regarded as fast for its time. A modern laptop or smartphone works at about 20 or 30 million times the speed.

Sadly, the machine in the museum is not the original, although it incorporates some historic components. It's a full-size replica, made for the 50th anniversary of the discovery. The original Baby was designed as a testbed: it was almost immediately cannibalised to build a more practical model, the Manchester Mark 1. This became the basis of the Ferranti Mark 1, the world's first commercially available general-purpose computer, put on sale in 1951.

Address Science and Industry Museum, Liverpool Road, Manchester M3 4FP, +44 (0)161 832 2244, www.scienceandindustrymuseum.org.uk | **Getting there** Free bus (route 1) to Lower Byrom Street | **Hours** Daily 10am–5pm | **Tip** A short walk away at 33a Collier Street is the Saul Hay Gallery, a private gallery where you can see exhibitions of contemporary art.

68 Manchester Jewish Museum
Look, listen, learn and eat

There's a new arrival on Cheetham Hill Road, once the thriving home of Manchester's Jewish community and now a grungy stretch of car parts and cash and carry shops. It looks striking with its laser-cut Corten steel cladding, perforated with star-shaped patterns echoing the design of the Victorian Spanish and Portuguese synagogue next door, the only complete synagogue left in the area. Together the two buildings form the Manchester Jewish Museum. The stories it tells are relevant to our own time for Jews and non-Jews alike: stories of successive waves of immigration, of peoples forced to leave their homes and make new lives, starting from humble beginnings and ending up as valued citizens, moving from one part of the city to another, establishing their own schools, shops and businesses.

You can visit the splendidly restored synagogue and see its stained-glass windows, the reading desk and the precious scrolls of the torah in the ark. There is also plenty to see in the museum, but it is not all prayer shawls and skullcaps: the exhibits illustrate how Jewish people came to Manchester and what they did when they got here, with maps of where they lived, posters for Jewish entertainments, photographs of Jewish shops, raincoats made in Jewish factories and samples of leather made in a Jewish tannery. At the heart of this museum are the stories of individuals told in their own words. Here, oral history comes into its own: pick up a speaker, hold it to your ear, and quite ordinary objects – a ticket, a notebook, a bag – movingly come to life when you listen to their owners talking. Food is also important: naturally, the café serves bagels and falafel, but schools and other groups can also book a session in the Learning Kitchen to bake, cook and eat together: a powerful way to experience Jewish heritage.

Address 190 Cheetham Hill Road, Manchester M8 8LW, +44 (0)161 834 9879, www.manchesterjewishmuseum.com | **Getting there** Bus 41 or 135 to Cheetham Hill Road/Derby Street | **Hours** Daily 10am–5pm, booking in advance advised | **Tip** Another relic of Victorian Cheetham Hill, on the other side of the road, is Cheetham Town Hall, with its pretty cast-iron *porte-cochère*. It is now an Indian restaurant and banqueting hall.

69 Manchester Poplars
As seen in St John's Gardens

Populus nigra betulifolia is currently Britain's most endangered tree, yet it got its name – 'Manchester Poplar' – a century ago for its exceptional resilience. At that time, a great many of Manchester's trees were dying, suffocated by layers of soot and acid pollution caused by coal burning in the city's factories, mills and dwellings. The pollutants damaged the leaves, reducing the trees' ability to photosynthesise and making them vulnerable to disease and pests. The native black poplar, however, was an exception, and its unique capacity to survive air pollution allowed it to thrive in Manchester's filthy air.

During the economic depression in the 1930s, when unemployment soared, Manchester Corporation devised a tree-planting scheme to create jobs. Men were hired to go out on bicycles with a bundle of poplar saplings and an iron bar, and wherever a suitable green area was found they made a hole and poked a little tree into the ground. This led to thousands of Manchester Poplars popping up on streets, verges, parks, fields and green spaces across the city. These tall, graceful trees became a distinctive local feature, with their rough, grey bark, downy green leaves and their habit of leaning to one side.

Sadly, the tree is no longer a common sight, for unlike other black poplars, the Manchester sub-species is seriously threatened by poplar scab disease, a virus that can lead to the death of the tree within five years. There is no effective treatment and, since the Manchester trees come from one clone, there is no genetic diversity. In the year 2000, it was estimated that around 5,000 remained in the city, mostly from the 1930s mass planting, although many had already been felled in later slum clearance programmes. Now few remain, and the two fine specimens in St John's Gardens, dominating the little park with their height and spread, are rare survivors.

Address St John's Gardens, Lower Byrom Street, Manchester M3 4AP | **Getting there** Free bus (route 1) to Quay Street | **Hours** Accessible 24 hours | **Tip** There is also a green look to the high-level Deansgate-Castlefield tram stop – it is surrounded by a living wall and wildflowers are encouraged to pop up between the tram tracks in summer.

70__Marble Arch
Pub with a theatrical touch

This local boozer on the otherwise drab Rochdale Road has all you could want of the great British pub. Dating from 1888, it was designed by Alfred Darbyshire, whose skill as a Manchester theatre architect (he designed the Palace Theatre) is revealed in the colourful interior. The bar is decked out in ceramic tiles, with a fireproof ceiling of glazed bricks supported on cast-iron beams and a lettered frieze listing the drinks consumed by its thirsty Victorian customers: ales, porters, whiskies, brandies and more. Light pours in through tall Gothic windows and shimmers on the tiles and the shelves of bottles. A mosaic floor adds gaiety, but there is something strange: it slopes down, drawing you on towards the bar and the temptations of liquor.

The drinks indeed are tempting, for the pub has its own beers; Marble Brewery was established at the rear in 1997, but now has premises nearby and a growing reputation. A range of their classic ales, including Manchester Bitter, Earl Grey IPA and Lagonda, as well as more esoteric brews such as chocolate and hazelnut stout (at 15% abv), are served from nine hand pumps on the bar, as well as eight selected keg lines.

Also exceptional is the food, traditional pub fare with a difference. People come here for the beer poached pork, apple and sage sausages and the Arch Pie filled with Marble stout-marinated featherblade steak, drunken onion and boozy gravy. There are veggie options, and specials are usually available. The artisan cheeseboard gives you a choice of 3, 6, 9 or 12 cheeses, and Marble Puddings include baked Basque cheesecake with honey and saffron poached pear, and white and dark chocolate brownie. Marble Sunday Roasts, available from noon until they're gone, are for those with voracious appetites. At the back is a paved backyard with chairs and tables, a sun trap in summer. Dog and child friendly, with super-helpful staff, this is a pub that you cannot miss.

Address 73 Rochdale Road, Manchester M4 4HY, +44 (0)161 832 5914, www.marblebeers.com | **Getting there** Bus 17, 118, 119 to Rochdale Road/Gould Street | **Hours** Mon, Wed & Thu noon–10pm, Fri & Sat noon–11pm, Sun noon–8pm | **Tip** Down Angel Street off Rochdale Road is One Angel Square, headquarters of the Co-operative Group. Shaped, like a sliced egg, the building makes maximum use of solar energy and is one of the greenest in the UK, designed to be flexible, sustainable and carbon-free.

71 Mark Addy Memorial
The people's hero

Salford's Weaste Cemetery contains the mortal remains of many of the city's greatest worthies, including Joseph Brotherton, Salford's first MP; Sir Charles Hallé, founder of the Hallé Orchestra; and Ferdinand Stanley, who was immortalised in Tennyson's epic poem 'The Charge of the Light Brigade'. But the most poignant memorial is to Mark Addy, a boatman who spent his life on the banks of the polluted River Irwell.

When he died in 1890, aged 52, he had saved the lives of more than 50 people from drowning. His first rescue, at the age of 13, before he could swim, was a small boy whom he dragged ashore with the aid of a plank. After marrying in 1860, he became licensee of the Old Boathouse Inn in Everard Street, where he was on hand should anyone get into difficulties in the waters. Some of those he rescued were reluctant to be saved, including a woman who had thrown herself into the river after her husband drowned. Another was a 17-stone woman who was suffering from *delirium tremens* caused by alcohol withdrawal and put up a spirited struggle; she was later committed to a mental asylum.

His final rescue was of a boy who had fallen into an especially polluted part of the river where many sewers discharged. After diving in three times, Addy saved the boy, but having swallowed a quantity of filthy water, he contracted tuberculosis, took to his bed and never recovered. Such was the grief at his passing that a memorial fund was established, which was so successful that in addition to the splendid granite obelisk, sufficient money remained for a silver rowing cup and annual competition held in his memory, and an oil portrait. This hangs in the Salford Art Gallery and shows our hero weighed down by a large quantity of decorations presented to him for bravery, the greatest accolade being the Albert Medal of the First Class, conferred by the Queen.

Address Cemetery Road, Salford M5 5NR, +44 (0)161 686 7290 | Getting there Bus 33 to Kirkham Street, Weaste and 7-minute walk or tram to Weaste (blue line) and 10-minute walk | Hours Apr–Sept 8am–8pm, Oct–Mar 8am–6pm | Tip Take a look at Collier Street Baths in Greengate, Salford's historic centre, where Mark Addy learned to swim. It is a sorry sight, for the handsome Italianate-style building is shamefully abandoned and ruinous.

72 Mayfield Park
From Grot Spot to Green Space

Manchester's first new park for over 100 years opened to universal acclaim in September 2022. It occupies what was a derelict industrial site in the city centre that has been transformed into an urban park that is not only for people, but for wildlife and plants, providing habitats and enhancing biodiversity in an area that was previously barren. The park is also unique in being the first phase of a wider commercial development.

As you enter, the first thing you see is the River Medlock meandering through the landscape. It was once the key to the site's industrial past, serving the Mayfield Print Works, established in 1782 and celebrated for its purple dye used in calico printing, and the Britannia Brewery, which opened in 1830. But for the last 50 years, the river was hidden underground. Now reopened, it acts as a flood plain together with the parkland to protect the city in times of heavy rain. Already kingfishers and herons have been spotted on the riverbanks.

The former Mayfield Station, used as a Postal Depot in its latter days, forms the backdrop to the park, and its industrial character sets the theme. Building materials and artefacts from across the site were salvaged and reused to create the river bridges and retaining walls. Purple flowering plants were chosen as a memory of the calico dye, and there are 40 species of tree, selected to suit the changing climate. During construction, 13 wells dating from the Victorian era were unearthed, three of which remain in use to irrigate the plants and trees. At the centre is the Mayfield Lawn, an event space that can be illuminated at night. But the climax is the adventure play area with eight shiny, metal towers linked by bridges and slides, evoking the factory chimneys that formerly surrounded the site. Local children were given first go on these space-age towers when the park opened. Their verdict: 'So scary!'

Address Boardman Gate Entrance, Mayfield Park, Baring Street, Manchester, M1 2PY, www.mayfieldpark.com | **Getting there** Tram (most lines) to Piccadilly and 5-minute walk | **Hours** Dawn to dusk | **Tip** At the heart of Depot Mayfield, alongside the park, is Freight Island, where you'll find bars, restaurants, food trucks and entertainment, Fri 4pm–midnight, Sat noon–midnight, Sun noon–10pm.

73 Minut Men
Concrete totems of the sixties

'What the hell are they?' said Prince Philip on seeing the three giant sculptures outside the new Salford Technical College (now Salford University) that he had come to open in 1967. Well known for putting his foot in it, this time the Prince had a point, as the sculptor William Mitchell never gave them a name. Are they animals, men, monsters or robots? From whichever angle you look at them, they have an uncanny presence, with faces and arms emerging from the angular jumble of shapes.

Mitchell specialised in working with concrete, which was disdained by most sculptors of the sixties as a building material and not a medium for fine art. He made a virtue of the roughness of concrete, creating an enormous variety of textures and relief patterns, sometimes mixing in crunchy bits of stone or inlaying pieces of mosaic and Victorian coloured tile to catch the eye. Mitchell tinted the concrete for each sculpture differently and each has a distinctive character but you can't pin them down. They glower on a grey day or catch the morning and evening sun, as they were carefully positioned to do, with shadows and highlights changing with the light and weather.

'I don't give a hoot if you don't like them, just as long as you look at them,' said Mitchell. He hoped to provoke the students: 'I want them to talk about them, laugh at them, even grumble at them. I want Salford people to have a share in them too.' Which they do, as the sculptures, visible from buses and cars passing on the A6, have become landmarks in an otherwise grim cityscape. In view of their ambiguous and indefinable nature, it is not surprising that over the years, students have given them various nicknames – Totem Poles; Faith, Hope and Charity; Freeman, Hardy and Willis (after a long-disappeared but once well-known chain of shoe shops) but the name that has stuck is the Minut Men.

Address Outside the Allerton Building, Frederick Road Campus, University Road, Salford M6 6PU | Getting there Train to Salford Crescent and 5-minute walk | Hours Accessible 24 hours | Tip Another striking work by William Mitchell is the giant mural behind the staircase inside the Mercure Hotel, Piccadilly, made of resin, bits of old piano and recycled bottle tops.

74__The Monastery
Lifting the spirits

There are many stories of threatened buildings rising like the proverbial phoenix from the ashes, but few match that of The Monastery. It begins with the arrival in Gorton in 1861 of a group of Franciscan friars from Belgium to help the poor of the area. Their ambition was to mark the triumphant return of the Franciscans after 320 years of persecution by erecting a friary and a parish church larger than any built in England since the Reformation. Their architect was Edward Welby Pugin, whose soaring west front and lofty interior are unforgettable. The church was completed in 10 years and by 1901 there were 6,000 parishioners.

But its glory was short-lived, for from the 1960s Gorton suffered catastrophic decline. The closure of local industries led to high unemployment, slum clearance and depopulation. Church attendance plummeted, and in 1989 the Franciscans closed up and departed. A property developer acquired the building, stripping it of its contents and selling off the land, before going bankrupt. Vandals caused huge damage, fires broke out and water poured in through the roofs. Without the action of a former altar boy, Paul Griffiths and his wife Elaine, it could have been the end. Elaine gave up her job to start a campaign, and by force of will gained support from the prestigious World Monument Fund. In time, EU and lottery money came in, and work began on reversing the decline. It has been a long and arduous job, not only reroofing and structural work but also restoring the spectacular high altar, and conserving the stolen statues of saints that turned up in an auction sale. Today, the monastery is open to visitors from Sunday to Thursday and holds numerous events including wellness activities, workshops, shows, markets and concerts. When the King, then Prince Charles, visited in 2010 he was overwhelmed, saying 'I find that just being here lifts my spirits and makes me feel that anything is possible.'

Address The Monastery, Gorton Lane, Manchester M12 5WF, +44 (0)161 233 3211, www.themonastery.co.uk | Getting there Bus 205 to The Monastery, or train to Gorton and 5-minute walk | Hours Sun–Thu 10am–4pm | Tip One mile to the east on Hyde Road, in the churchyard of the Brookfield Unitarian Church, is a splendid Gothic mausoleum to Richard Peacock, founder of the famous steam locomotive manufacturer Beyer, Peacock and Co.

75 the modernist
Celebrating brutalism

Tucked away in a minor street in the Northern Quarter, *the modernist* is home to a 'loose collaboration of dilettantes, artists, designers, architects, geographers, historians and enthusiasts' for modernist and brutalist architecture and design.

Started in Manchester in 2009, this community collective is spreading its influence across the country, with branches in several other British cities. The faintly anorakish group goes misty-eyed at the sight of concrete bunkers, and nostalgic about multistorey car parks, power stations and tower blocks. They curate exhibitions on urban planning, outdoor sculpture, motorways and life in the 1950s. Their stylish magazine is published quarterly and includes insights into the world of modernist design and titbits from the recent past you thought you had forgotten.

As well as a gallery for exhibitions and talks, there is a small shop where you can buy books, posters of Rochdale Bus Station, the demolished Hulme Crescents and the Merseyway Shopping Centre in Stockport; David Mellor cutlery, Mepal tableware and T-shirts celebrating four iconic female designers. There are also pin badges – brutalist, Futurist, modernist or minimalist, whatever you fancy; the badge for Windscale Nuclear Power Station glows in the dark.

One of the organisation's patrons, a committed badge-wearer, is the former Smiths guitarist Johnny Marr, whose New Town Velocity video features him wandering around Manchester's concrete buildings; clearly a kindred spirit judging from his immortal words 'I've been to a lot of cities in the UK and most of the houses I've seen look shit.' Another is the provocative journalist and TV presenter Jonathan Meades, whose style is blisteringly brutal. Ironically this shrine to modernism occupies a modest two-storey early 19th-century house with a Victorian shopfront, tastefully painted dark green.

Address 58 Port Street, Manchester M1 2EQ, www.the-modernist.org | **Getting there** 5 minute-walk from Piccadilly Gardens | **Hours** Tue–Sat 11am–5pm | **Tip** The *Daily Express* Building, a favourite of the modernist clique, designed by Sir Owen Williams and dating from 1939, can be seen on Great Ancoats Street, a 5-minute walk away.

76 Monument to Vimto
Have you got the bottle?

Remember Vimto? The purple fruit cordial of idyllic childhood summers is not just a memory. Vimto is still very much around today – you can even get Vimto ice lollies and jellybeans. Yet how many people know that Vimto began in Manchester, and that it continues to be one of Manchester's big success stories?

In 1908 John Noel Nichols, a wholesaler of herbs, spices and medicines, mixed the first batch at 19 Granby Row, Manchester and promoted it as a temperance drink with health benefits: the original name was Vim Tonic. The business grew rapidly and moved first to Salford, then to Old Trafford, then to Wythenshawe and Haydock Park; manufacture is now outsourced to several different sites. But that is only part of the story.

Starting in 1928–29, when the first exports went to British Guyana and then to India, Vimto has expanded internationally on a vast scale, and is now manufactured in 30 countries and sold in 85. The non-alcoholic drink has become wildly popular in the Middle East where alcohol is forbidden to the devout: Vimto is the preferred drink for the sunset feast during the holy fasting month of Ramadan. It's sweeter over there, because when it was originally exported, it was cheaper to transport in concentrated form. Now, over 20 million bottles a year are produced for the Gulf States alone, and millions more for the rest of the world. Back in Manchester, the exact spot where the first batch was made is a green space near Manchester University's Sackville Street building (the old Technical School). The purple potion is commemorated by a monument carved from sustainable wood in 1992 by Kerry Morrison: a gigantic Vimto bottle surrounded by luscious coloured fruits, the grapes, raspberries and blackcurrants that, combined with an undisclosed mix of 23 fruit essences, herbs and spices, make up the secret recipe that gives Vimto its unique taste.

Address Vimto Park, Granby Row, Manchester M1 3BU | **Getting there** Free bus (routes 1 or 2) to Aytoun Street | **Hours** Accessible 24 hours | **Tip** Eureka! Under the railway arches on nearby Altrincham Street is a statue of Archimedes in his bath.

77 Mr Lowry's Stockport
Dominated by the viaduct

The painter L. S. Lowry lived in Mottram-in-Longdendale, about 10 miles from Stockport. He was fascinated by Stockport's unique topography. The town centre is all up and down – it was built on sloping land, with the different levels linked by steeply rising streets, ramps and flights of stone steps. One of the streets, Underbank, is crossed by a bridge carrying another of the main streets high above it, with the Market Hall and the Parish Church at the upper level. From there, narrow cobbled alleyways run back down to the lower part of the town.

Stockport became an industrial centre in the 19th century with factories and chimneys everywhere, but the standout structure is the blackened brick railway viaduct. It is an unforgettable sight towering above the river, dominating the approaches to the town from all directions, and glimpsed between buildings or down steps as you walk through the old centre. When built in 1839–40 it was the largest railway viaduct in the world, its 24 arches striding solemnly across the valley 111 feet (33.8 metres) above the river, taking the trains over the soot-black factories.

Lowry drew or painted a few specific views of Stockport – the viaduct, the staircases and steep Crowther Street, with typical Lowry people climbing up and down the slope between the houses (the picture is in the Stockport Art Gallery). Sadly, the street now looks completely different as it has been rebuilt. In contrast, the railway viaduct has hardly changed: it is now a listed building.

Most of Lowry's industrial panoramas are not views of real places, but imaginary scenes incorporating memories of the things he had seen in different locations. Tall arched viaducts, dwarfing the surrounding buildings, are a haunting presence in many of his paintings. For Lowry, the viaduct became an archetype that was central to his unique vision of the industrial North.

Address Stockport Town Centre | Getting there Train to Stockport | Tip The art gallery at The Lowry, Salford, has a large permanent exhibition of Lowry paintings.

78   Mr Thomas's Chop House
Manchester's first gastropub

This Manchester institution, founded in 1867 by Thomas Studd, announces itself on Cross Street with an exuberantly decorated façade in buff-coloured terracotta and red brick. It is so narrow that it looks as though it has been squashed in between its more sober neighbours. The building dates from 1901: the front part, now the bar, was originally a shop, but beyond it is the original chop house dining room, a long and narrow space lined with green and cream tiles. It has an authentic turn-of-the-century atmosphere – fortunately it hasn't been poshed up with white tablecloths or fancy props and the service is friendly and informal.

Mr Thomas's specialises in traditional hearty fare – steaks, chops, burgers and pies – but this is no ordinary pub grub. The Chop House is a first-class restaurant with cooking by top chefs who care about taste, quality ingredients and careful preparation; the menus vary with the season and include imaginative modern touches. The corned beef hash – definitely not out of a tin – is a secret recipe that takes 10 days to prepare. It's made with chives and comes with crispy bacon and an oozy soft-boiled egg on top.

If you think steamed suet pudding might weigh on the stomach try the Chop House daily pie – it is positively luscious, with tender slow-cooked meats inside a soft and delicious suet casing, accompanied by lashings of gravy and mushy peas. Other choices might include chicken supreme or the posh ham, egg and chips, which consists of brown sugar and orange juice glazed bacon chops with pan-fried duck egg and confit potato chips. Sunday lunch with roast beef and Yorkshire pudding is a speciality. There is an excellent wine list – the award-winning Sommelier George Bergier learned his trade at Manchester's legendary Midland French. Finish off with sticky toffee pudding, apple and blackberry crumble or the Great Lancastrian cheeseboard – and loosen your belt.

Address 52 Cross Street, Manchester M2 7AR, +44 (0)161 832 2245, www.tomschophouse.com | **Getting there** Free bus (routes 1 or 2) to King Street | **Hours** Mon–Thu noon–10.30pm, Fri & Sat noon–11pm, Sun noon–10pm | **Tip** Inside the doorway of 20 St Ann's Square, the wall is papered with a fascinating map of late Victorian Manchester.

79 National Cycling Centre
Sport, speed and centrifugal force

At first sight, the steep banking to the race track at the Manchester Velodrome looks incredibly dangerous – why don't the cyclists topple over and fall down to the bottom in a chaotic heap? Yet as they sweep by, sometimes leaning at perilous angles, you will be mesmerised by the seemingly effortless speed and tactical moves of the participants in this compelling sport. The National Cycling Centre was established in east Manchester in 1994 with the opening of the country's first indoor Olympic track. At first, it was dismissed as a white elephant, but in its short life it has hosted many international championships and become the home of the Tour de France-winning UK Team Sky. It is used every day from early morning to late at night by both professional cyclists and members of the public. Described by *Cycling Weekly* as the 'beating heart of British Cycling's ascension to the top of world cycling,' it has seen world records set and has a reputation for the quality of its track.

Alongside the velodrome is an indoor BMX track, which also caters for riders new to the sport as well as world-class athletes. The Elite Track begins with the only eight-metre start hill in the UK leading to a challenging range of jumps and turns. Close by is the outdoor Clayton Vale BMX Track, which offers thrills as well as challenges.

For those with little or no experience of track cycling, there are taster sessions in the velodrome (children must be 12 years or over), including events for families. The centre is open to spectators at all times (free except for major events), with seating for 3,500 people beneath the great arched roof that allows unobstructed views. And why the need for such steep banking? It's physics, stupid. Combatting the effect of centrifugal force, it prevents the cyclists from sliding off the track, saves them from falling over, and allows them to keep their speed while turning.

Address Velodrome, Stuart Street, Manchester M11 4DQ, +44 (0)161 233 2244, www.nationalcyclingcentre.com | **Getting there** Tram to Velopark (blue line) and 5-minute walk | **Hours** Mon–Fri 7.30am–10pm, Sat & Sun 7.30am–7pm, check website for events | **Tip** A 10-minute walk away, on Ashton New Road, is Clayton Hall, a 16th-century moated house with a stone bridge across the moat. It opens two Saturdays a month, except Dec and Jan; for dates check www.claytonhall.org.

80 Ordsall Hall
Old house, new garden

It is a miracle that Ordsall Hall has survived. One of the finest half-timbered manor houses in the region, it used to be a prominent sight, set in green fields outside the small market town of Salford. Later engulfed by rows of terraced housing and industrial buildings, it was all but forgotten. Now it has been beautifully restored and an imaginatively designed garden has been created for it.

The hall was the home of the Radcliffes, a leading Lancashire family. Parts of the structure, which was surrounded by a moat, date from the 14th century, but in about 1510 the main part of the house was rebuilt with the attractive quatrefoil (four-leaf) timber patterning that makes the exterior so appealing. Brick extensions followed in the 17th century and the north side was rebuilt in the late Victorian period. By this time, the moat had been filled in and the Radcliffes had long gone. After a chequered history, Ordsall Hall became a museum in 1972 and, following major repairs, it reopened in 2011. Grimy brickwork was cleaned, and the thick black paint on the decorative timberwork was removed to reveal the natural colour of the wood. Inside is the Great Hall with a spectacular timber roof and a lofty bay window alcove. Beyond is the Parlour, with gold stars on the ceiling; it houses a richly carved bed, the only piece of furniture in the house known to have belonged to the Radcliffes. Each room has activities for children based on daily life at Ordsall in the past.

Outside there are two acres of organically managed gardens; they include an orchard with historic fruit varieties, a herb garden with medieval and Tudor herbs and a formal garden with clipped yews and low box hedges enclosing drifts of santolina and lavender. There is even a World War I allotment recreated as part of the centenary commemorations, to reflect the wartime use of the grounds for allotments.

Address 322 Ordsall Lane, Ordsall, Salford M5 3AN, +44 (0)161 686 7440, https://ordsallhall.com | **Getting there** Tram to Exchange Quay (blue orange line) and 12-minute walk | **Hours** Mon–Thu 10am–4pm, Sun 11.30am–4pm | **Tip** Wythenshawe Hall (www.wythenshawehall.org), another fine half-timbered house, suffered from a fire in 2016 and opens one Sunday a month, check website for details.

81 The Pankhurst Centre
Where the suffragette movement began

Between 1898 and 1907, 62 Nelson Street was home to Emmeline Pankhurst and her family. In 1903, a small group of women met here and formed the Women's Social and Political Union, soon to be known as the suffragettes. The suffragettes fought for women's right to vote using militant tactics, attacking policemen, smashing windows and chaining themselves to railings, where more respectable methods of protest had failed. The women persisted in the face of public ridicule, enduring imprisonment and going on hunger strike to draw attention to their cause. They suspended their campaign during World War I, but in 1918 women over 30 who owned property were given the vote and in 1928 it was extended to all women over 21.

Inside the house is a reconstruction of the parlour where the meeting was held, and there are displays about the suffragette movement, including a short film showing them in action. There is a café, an exhibition area and the volunteer guides are enthusiastic and knowledgeable. The museum shares the house and the one next door with Manchester Women's Aid, which supports women suffering from domestic violence and abuse. There is also a small garden with metal sculptures on the theme of votes for women.

The two elegant Georgian houses are dwarfed by a multistorey car park and surrounded by other anonymous buildings associated with the Manchester Royal Infirmary. It is shocking that no attempt was made to relate these blocks in scale, materials or design to the two surviving historic houses. In the 1960s, the houses had become derelict and the hospital authorities thought they could get rid of them – even though their national significance in the history of democratic reform was well known. It was only after a long struggle by conservationists and women's organisations that the houses were saved. Just like the suffragettes, they never gave up – and they won.

Address 60–62 Nelson Street, Manchester M13 9WP, +44 (0)161 273 5673, www.pankhurstmuseum.com | **Getting there** Bus 15, 18, 42, 142, 191 to Nelson Street | **Hours** Thu & Sun 11am–4pm | **Tip** *Rise Up, Women*, a posthumous statue of Emmeline Pankhurst by Hazel Reeves, stands in St Peter's Square in the city centre.

82 Peterloo Memorial
Manchester's massacre of the innocents

On 16 August, 1819, more than 60,000 people from across the Manchester region gathered in St Peter's Fields to demand fair political representation. Dressed in their Sunday best, they brought their children with them, eager to hear the words of Henry 'Orator' Hunt, the leader of the national parliamentary reform movement. A few minutes after Hunt started speaking, without warning, the crowd was attacked by armed men on horseback with indiscriminate force. Eighteen people died and almost 700 were seriously injured, more than 200 with sabre wounds; many were women and some were children. Known first as the 'Manchester massacre', it soon acquired the title Peterloo, recalling the blood shed on the battlefield of Waterloo four years earlier. It was an atrocity made all the more serious for its backing by the local magistrates, and ultimately by the government. To reformers it came to symbolise Tory callousness and despotism.

Two hundred years after the event, a fitting memorial was erected close to where the massacre took place. Designed by Turner Prize-winning artist Jeremy Deller, it is a circular stepped structure, redolent of a burial mound. Beautifully cut into the stone, and facing outwards in the direction of where they came from, are the names of the people who took part, and the towns around Manchester they represented. The horizontal surfaces of the steps are inlaid with images associated with Peterloo, and the top of the memorial makes reference to other state attacks on peaceful civilian protests, including Tiananmen Square and Bloody Sunday. Many different stones from across the UK have been used to create the memorial, their bright colours recalling the banners held up by those demanding social reform. Intended as a gathering point for protest, it embodies the spirit of radicalism that remains a part of the city's identity.

Address Windmill Street, Manchester M2 3DL | **Getting there** Tram to St Peter's Square (all lines) | **Hours** Accessible 24 hours | **Tip** The large building behind the memorial is known as Manchester Central, and is the city's conference and exhibition centre. It was built as a railway station in 1880.

83 Peveril of the Peak
Here's to Nancy

Standing like a TARDIS amidst large Victorian warehouses and modern office blocks, this characterful little pub with tiled walls in striking tones of green and orange holds its own. Venture inside and you will be not be disappointed, for it is a traditional pub through and through. A choice of drinking spaces around an island bar awaits you: the tiled corridor with polished mahogany screen inset with coloured glass; the public bar with antique table football machine, bell pushes on the wall and a long bar counter; the snug (formerly the smoke room) with cast-iron fireplace and entertaining pictures such as the Gay Photographer (a Victorian sheet music cover) and a 1960s jigsaw of a café interior with pop ephemera; and the L-shaped back bar with pool table. All have fixed seating around the walls with well-worn, comfy moquette upholstery. Quality beers are always on tap including Titanic Plum Porter, Timothy Taylor and Brightside.

The name of the pub is a tribute to the now-vanished popularity of the novels of Sir Walter Scott, whose *The Peveril of the Peak* set in 17th-century Derbyshire was published in 1823, seven years before the first record of the pub. The external tilework and much of the interior décor, however, was installed around 1900. Traditional pubs like this are a dying breed, but 'the Pev' is truly exceptional, for it has been in the hands of the same landlady for well over 50 years. Nancy Swanick took over in January 1971 and, supported by her son and cellarman Maurice, she has no intention of leaving. No wonder she has attracted a band of loyal supporters. Nancy treats them as her family, and their banter and impromptu sing-songs provide a homely atmosphere. Over the years, she has fought off attempts to take the pub away from her, such as when in the 1980s it was threatened with demolition for a road scheme. Long may she reign.

Address 127 Great Bridgewater Street, Manchester M1 5JQ, +44 (0)161 236 6364 | **Getting there** Tram to St Peter's Square (all lines) and 5-minute walk | **Hours** Mon–Thu noon–11pm, Fri & Sat noon–midnight, Sun noon–10.30pm | **Tip** For those intent on a pub crawl, continue on to The Briton's Protection at 50 Great Bridgewater Street, worth a stop for the quality of its historic interior, its beer and the panoply of whiskies.

84 Plaza Cinema
Stockport's silver screen

Settle into your seat, upholstered in deep blue and gold moquette, as the house lights go down, and with a glorious crescendo the mighty Compton organ rises out of the floor filling the auditorium with sound, the backlit console decorated with sunburst motifs that change colour as the organist plays. It could be 1932, when the Plaza Cinema Stockport first opened as the last word in Art Deco luxury, with jazz-styled gold- and silver-tinted décor, a full orchestra pit and a smart café with waitresses in white pinnies serving dainty teas. But it isn't the thirties, it's now. Unlike most super-cinemas, the Plaza survived three decades of bingo, and today the café is back in action and the organ is thrilling the audience again.

The Plaza was lucky. With cinemas everywhere closing down or being divided into smaller units, the Plaza became a rarity, and in 1997 its importance was recognised by English Heritage, which awarded it a Grade II listing, later upgraded to Grade II*. In 1999, the bingo finally stopped and the Plaza was forced to close, but it was rescued by locals who founded a trust to purchase and preserve it.

The cinema reopened in 2000 and a major £3.2 million restoration programme was carried out in 2009 to remedy the worst of the vandalism of the bingo years when seats had been ripped out, floor rakes flattened and colour schemes changed. Today, the restored cream-tiled façade is transformed at night with spectacular red and green neon, while inside authentic lighting effects have been recreated, all the seats have been reinstated to the original design, and the landscape murals in the auditorium have been repainted. Run by a small staff, with a host of volunteers, the Plaza plays to packed houses with a programme of live shows, musicals, concerts, comedians, pantomimes and classic films shown – as they should be seen – on the big screen.

Address Mersey Square, Stockport SK1 1SP, +44 (0)161 477 7779, www.stockportplaza.co.uk | **Getting there** Train to Stockport and 8-minute walk | **Hours** Café Wed–Sat 11am–3pm | **Tip** You might find some Art Deco at Agapanthus Interiors, 77 Wellington Street, worth visiting for its vast range of antique light fittings of all periods.

85 Police Museum
A night in the slammer

Truncheons, handcuffs, murder weapons... there are lots of fascinating – and gruesome – things to see in this riveting small museum, but there are two things that make it special: the building and the volunteers. The building is a real police station, a modest red-brick structure dating from 1879. Parts have been altered but there are some authentic interiors so atmospheric that they often crop up in films and TV police dramas.

The charge office, with its big wooden counter, is where you would go to report a crime to the duty officer – and if you were apprehended, it was where you would be taken to be charged. Leading off it is a tiled corridor of grim police cells, where drunks and petty offenders were held overnight before being taken before the magistrates at the courtrooms in nearby Minshull Street. On a busy night, the cells, designed for 2 people, were sometimes crammed with as many as 16. Originally there were no toilets in the cells, only a bucket (yuk... let's not go there).

As for the volunteers, most of them are retired police officers and they bring the displays to life with entertaining stories from history or from their own experience. They offer you helmets and body armour to try on, they demonstrate the different types of handcuffs and explain how communications have changed from ear-shattering police whistles and rattles, via the brick-like walkie-talkies of the 1960s to today's lightweight electronic radios with built-in GPS. You can also see police motorbikes and scooters; a magistrates' courtroom rescued from a demolished police station and rebuilt; equipment for forging coins and banknotes; wreckage from the Strangeways Prison riots; off-putting exhibits from famous murder cases; and a terrifying selection of confiscated weapons including machetes, knuckle-dusters and metal piping. Now – was it Colonel Mustard in the Library?

Address Greater Manchester Police Museum, 57A Newton Street, Manchester M1 1ET, +44 (0)161 856 3284, www.gmpmuseum.co.uk | **Getting there** 5 minute-walk from Piccadilly Gardens | **Hours** Tue 10.30am–4pm | **Tip** Round the corner at 37 Lever Street, Fred Aldous sells everything you could possibly require for arts and crafts from crochet and candle making to watercolours and woodcraft.

86 Portico Library
Hidden literary oasis

The Portico Library is named after the most striking feature of its elegant neoclassical frontage, but if you enter through the portico you will find yourself in a pub. The library used to occupy the whole building, with a lofty central room two storeys high topped by a glass dome. Sadly, the space has been divided horizontally, and the library now occupies only the top half, although the Library has announced an ambitious plan to open up the space again. For the time being you go in a little door around the corner in Charlotte Street and walk up a shabby stone staircase (there is no lift).

Once in the library, however, you can savour one of the most atmospheric interiors in Manchester. There are books everywhere, with bookcases lining the walls, and gold lettering spelling out 'Voyages and Travel', 'Biographies and History' and 'Polite Literature' (the latter meaning novels, poetry and drama suitable for polite society, that is the educated classes).

The library opened in 1806 when Manchester was expanding rapidly because of the cotton trade but had few cultural activities: originally styled the Portico Library and Newsroom, it stocked not only the latest books but over 100 newspapers, journals and magazines, including the London papers. The first secretary was Peter Mark Roget, inventor of the thesaurus, a compendium of words arranged in groups of similar meaning. He started to write it here in Manchester but left after two years. Famous members included Robert Peel senior, Richard Cobden, John Dalton, the Revd William Gaskell, husband of the novelist Elizabeth Gaskell (women were not allowed to join in those days) and Eric Cantona.

For years the Portico was a members-only subscription library. Although you still have to pay a fee to get the latest books and use the private reading room, today the main part of the library, including a café, is open to the public and admission is free.

Address 57 Mosley Street, Manchester M3 3HY, +44 (0)161 236 6785, www.theportico.org.uk | **Getting there** Tram to St Peter's Square (all lines) | **Hours** Mon–Wed 10am–5pm, Thu 10am–7pm, Fri 11am–5 pm, Sat noon–4pm | **Tip** For another literary connection walk down to the corner of Cross Street and John Dalton Street. A plaque records the birthplace of Thomas de Quincey, author of *Confessions of an English Opium Eater*.

87 Post Box, Corporation Street
It survived the IRA bomb

It was just an ordinary red pillar box like thousands of others. On a sunny Saturday morning 16 June, 1996, a van parked by a letter box outside Marks & Spencer on Corporation Street. Within three minutes a traffic warden had booked the van for parking on a double yellow line. About 15 minutes later, a caller with an Irish accent phoned Granada TV with a warning that a bomb on the corner of Corporation Street and Cannon Street would go off in an hour. The police sprang into action, clearing about 80,000 people from the area while experts tried to defuse the bomb by remote control. They ran out of time. At 11.20am the bomb went off with an explosion that could be heard 15 miles away, detonating 3,300 pounds of explosives, the largest bomb ever set off in mainland Britain.

Marks & Spencer, the Arndale Centre and an adjacent office block were wrecked, the domes of the Royal Exchange and Corn Exchange were badly damaged, the stained glass was blown out of the cathedral and windows were shattered in buildings all around. Over 200 people were injured, mainly by flying glass, although because of the prompt action of the police no one was killed. Remarkably, the post box was hardly damaged.

A few days later a postman was given permission to enter the stricken area. He stepped carefully through the heaps of rubble and broken glass, emptied the box and put the letters into his bag. They arrived at their destinations as if nothing had happened. Since then, old buildings were repaired, shiny new ones put up, and the area was improved and pedestrianised. The post box was removed, repainted and put back – not quite in its original position – a symbol of how Manchester survived one of the worst disasters ever, and got on with its business.

Address Corporation Street, Manchester near the Arndale Centre bridge | **Getting there** Tram to Exchange Square (pink or grey line) | **Tip** The historic half-timbered Sinclair's Oyster Bar and the Old Wellington Inn survived the blast but were dismantled and moved 300 metres northwards to a new site near the cathedral.

88 Private White V.C.
British craftsmanship at its best

Once there were hundreds of small factories in Manchester making raincoats. Today there is just one, Private White V.C. It produces upmarket high-quality men's outerwear – beautifully made waterproof coats, waxed jackets and Harrington jackets – plus knitwear and shirting. You can buy them online, and at select stores all over the world – but the unique thing about Private White is that you can tour the factory and see how the clothes are put together as well as buy them in the factory shop. It is a joy to go round the factory and see the traditional skills and the care and craftsmanship shown by the pattern-cutters, machinists and button stitchers. It comes as a surprise to learn that many of the textiles the company uses are British, some still woven in Lancashire; and that all the work is carried out on site without any outsourcing. Although the factory is within walking distance of Manchester city centre, it is in a run-down part of Salford – so it is equally astonishing that the only other Private White shop in the UK is at a fancy Mayfair address.

The company is named after Private Jack White, who was awarded the Victoria Cross for bravery during World War I. On leaving the army he went into the garment trade, eventually rising to own the factory, which has been making clothing since Victorian times – everything from military greatcoats to airline uniforms. Latterly the main business was making outerwear for Burberry, Aquascutum and other top British names, but the company's viability was threatened by the trend to move manufacturing abroad. Enter James Eden, White's great-grandson. He could see the potential of the old factory with its unbroken tradition of craft skills and its outstanding historical archive of sample garments; leaving his lucrative City job he came back North in 2010 and reinvented the family business as a luxury heritage brand.

Address Cottenham House, 1 Cottenham Lane, Manchester M3 7LJ, +44 (0)161 834 3062, www.privatewhitevc.com | **Getting there** Tram (most lines) or train to Victoria and 15-minute walk | **Hours** Mon–Thu 9am–5pm, Fri 9am–4pm, Sat 9am–1pm; booking essential | **Tip** Cross the footbridge outside the factory and on the walk back to Manchester you will pass another unique survival, the Manchester Tennis and Racquet Club, 33 Blackfriars Road, where real tennis is still played.

89 Richmond Tea Rooms
Through the looking glass

The Richmond Tea Rooms opens for breakfast and serves lunch but it's the afternoon tea that brings in the customers. Just look at those cakes – layers and layers of scrumptious sponge, soaked with lemon syrup or lashings of rich chocolate ganache alternating with crème pâtissière; luscious cream cheese frosting on the carrot cake, real Arabica in the coffee and walnut cake, and an eye-popping Gay Pride rainbow cake. There are a few healthy options – children's set teas include carrot and cucumber sticks with hummus as well as child-sized scones and dainty sandwiches, but most of the menu is given over to self-indulgence.

There's something else that people come here for – camp. The Richmond is only minutes away from the Gay Village and the over-the-top décor of the Tea Rooms exudes decadence. The interior has an Alice in Wonderland theme with touches of Salvador Dali – giant playing cards, oversized watches, hearts and diamonds wallpapers and *Eat Me* and *Drink Me* signs. There are red velvet buttoned chairs, lacy tablecloths, china cups and saucers in flowery and willow-pattern designs, heaps of exotic cushions, cascades of pink cherry blossom (artificial) and palm trees (real). Downstairs is the Enchanted Forest room, used for special events such as Burlesque Revues and Mad Hatter's Tea Parties with drag queens in attendance and double-entendres in abundance – strictly adults only, and the drinks are stronger than tea. The Queens Tea consists of finger sandwiches, a mini quiche and an assortment of cakes and scones. There are ice cream sundaes topped with whipped cream and foaming frappe milkshakes. If you feel in need of something less dainty, go for the Tweedles, which includes beer battered fish and skin-on chips and a homemade Cumberland scotch egg, as well as scones, sandwiches, tea and why not add a glass of bubbly? You won't need any supper.

Address 46 Sackville Street, Manchester M1 3WF, +44 (0)161 697 4474, www.richmondtearooms.com | Getting there Free bus (routes 1 or 2) to Chorlton Street; access difficult for wheelchair users (2 steps plus chairlift) | Hours Mon–Fri 10am–7pm, Sat 9am–8pm, Sun 9am–7pm | Tip In Sackville Gardens in front of the Tea Rooms is a statue of Alan Turing; the Beacon of Hope, a memorial to those living with and those who died of AIDS; and the National Transgender Remembrance Memorial.

90 Rochdale Town Hall
Municipal magnificence

Great medieval towns are renowned for their castles and churches. Victorian industrial towns expressed their wealth and pride by building town halls. Rochdale Town Hall, although smaller than the better-known Manchester Town Hall, is every bit as magnificent. With its steeply sloping roof, stepped gables and clock tower, it pays tribute to the medieval architecture of Flemish towns, which also became rich from textile manufacture.

From 2021-24, a major restoration of the building was carried out. Now you can see the fabulous interior with its colourful stencilled wall patterns, painted friezes and ceilings, glorious stained glass, tiled floors and intricate carvings. The Mayor's Parlour is decorated with leaves, flowers, birds, one of Aesop's fables and the motto '*In Vino Veritas*'. In the Council Chamber is a frieze of the history of textile manufacture starting with the Greeks and ending with a Rochdale mill girl at a mechanical loom. Climb the double staircase, lit by radiant heraldic windows, and the decoration comes to a climax in the Great Hall, with a superb hammer-beam roof carved with angels, an ornate organ and windows portraying British monarchs from William the Conqueror to Victoria. A mural painting depicts the signing of the Magna Carta.

The architect was W. H. Crossland, and the building opened in 1871. Some years later the tower caught fire. Even though the fire station was in the same building, the Rochdale fire brigade was reputedly so disorganised that the Oldham firemen arrived first, but they failed to save the tower, which was rebuilt to the design of Alfred Waterhouse, architect of Manchester Town Hall. In the Mayor's Reception Room, supporting the ceiling there are carved corbels of Crossland and the Mayor. By the time the building was complete, the cost had increased by eight times the original budget: across the room is another corbel of the Treasurer who is shaking his fist at the others.

Address The Esplanade, Rochdale OL16 1AB, +44 (0)170 692 4797, www.rochdale.gov.uk/townhall | **Getting there** Tram to Rochdale Town Centre (pink line) or train to Rochdale and 10-minute walk | **Hours** Daily 10am–4pm; check website for room closures due to private functions | **Tip** The council offices and library have moved to a new building at Number One Riverside, which has won numerous awards for its innovative, energy-efficient design.

91 Runaway Brewery
Behind the scenes at the microbrewery

Manchester's best beer can now be found alongside the River Mersey in Stockport, the Runaway Brewery having moved out of the city centre to larger premises. Here, the team Ollie, Jake and Mark continue their mission to brew by hand, and in small batches, beers of the highest quality: what they call 'modern British beer'. You can discover the secrets if you book a fascinating tour with generous tastings, a homely atmosphere and convivial chat.

Runaway, which was set up a decade ago, is as small as a brewery can be: it produces 5½ barrels (900 litres) at each brew, three times a week. Recently, the focus has changed to real ales (hand-pulled) in the traditional manner, including best bitter and ruby ale. The core range is complemented by regular favourites and specials resulting from collaborations with other brewers and beer fans to create unique ales. Among the favourites are the refreshing Pale Ale, the fruitier, multi award winning Indian Pale Ale, and the Extra Special Bitter (ESB) with its aroma of rich dried fruits. There is Dry Irish Stout with dark chocolate and roasted malt aromas, and the lighter Farmhouse Ale, a wheat beer brewed with Saaz and spelt. More experimental are the barrel-aged and blended beers such as the Tropical Stout that is aged in both rum and tequila barrels, or the Calder Valley Honey Stingo, a classic Yorkshire style, taking inspiration from the blended beers associated with Belgian brewing traditions.

As you will discover on the tour, this is a brewery that has rejected press-button controls. A passion for beer and a striving for quality is what motivates Ollie and his pals. Everything from the mash tank through the fermentation process to the bottling and labelling is hands-on. When you have finished the tour, you can chill out in the tap room, or in the courtyard during summer days, and sample a few more of the brews, for you won't find anything better than this.

Address 9-11 Astley Street, Stockport SK 1AW, www.therunawaybrewery.com | **Getting there** Train to Stockport and 10-minute walk | **Hours** Tap Room Thu 3–9.30pm, Fri & Sat 1–10pm; Bottle shop Mon–Fri 10am–4pm; Tours – booking essential | **Tip** Ye Olde Vic at 1 Chatham Street near Stockport Station is a traditional boozer with six handpumps that dispense an ever-changing range of guest beers. Open evenings only.

92 Salford Lads' Club
Not just for Smiths fans

The iconic cover photo for The Smiths' album *The Queen is Dead* taken in front of the Salford Lads' Club, is not the sole reason to seek it out. The club's history and its building are more important than that brief moment in time. Boys' clubs took hold in the Victorian period to provide an alternative to teenage street gangs, and several were set up in the most deprived parts of Manchester and Salford. The Salford Lads' Club, which is the only one left, was funded by James and William Groves, owners of the local brewery. The club was opened in 1904 by Chief Scout Baden-Powell, and provided sports, music and games; the club also held annual camping holidays in Wales. Since then 22,500 members have passed through, among them actor Albert Finney, Allan Clarke and Graham Nash of the 1960s pop band The Hollies, and footballer Eddie Colman. Every member's details, including their activities at the club and their first job are recorded in the extensive archive – nothing has been thrown away.

The building too is a remarkable survival, for it is almost completely unaltered. At the centre is a double-height gymnasium with a viewing gallery, and on the first floor is a concert hall with musicians' balcony. There is a boxing ring and a billiards room with original tables and benches. The Smiths' connection is celebrated with an eye-popping display of memorabilia, for while Stephen Wright's original photograph is now in the National Portrait Gallery, the Smiths' Room, formerly used for weightlifting, is plastered with posters and photos of the band, together with messages from visiting fans, covering walls, ceiling and hinged screens that swing out from the corners. Groups come from across the world to pay homage, write their messages, buy some of the coolest T-shirts you will find in Manchester from the gift shop, and take selfies on the sacred pavement outside.

Address Coronation Street, Salford M5 3RX, +44 (0)161 872 3767, www.salfordladsclub.org.uk | **Getting there** Bus 33 to Comus Street, Salford | **Hours** Wed & Sat 11am – 2pm | **Tip** Take a walk around the New Barracks Estate, Salford's first municipal housing scheme, centred on Regent Square. The club was built as an integral part, balanced at the other end of the street by St Ignatius Church.

93 Sifters

When Liam and Noel were still speaking

'Mr Sifter' became a star with the release of the Oasis number 'Shakermaker' where Liam Gallagher sings that Mr Sifter would sell him songs when he was just 16. Both Liam and his brother Noel were fans of this modest record shop in Burnage near the house in Cranwell Drive where they grew up, and 'Mr Sifter' – real name Peter Howard – is still there after selling songs for over 40 years. The name was a play on the art of sifting through records, and it stuck. Now Oasis fans travel from across the globe to admire this sage of the music scene, although Pete grins when he says 'Often they just come in and stare at me for 20 minutes and then bog off. It can be a bit embarrassing when I'm just standing there eating my sandwich.'

But there is a better reason for visiting Sifters, which is a gem of a record shop, selling old and new vinyls, CDs, DVDs, and even cassettes. The prices are more than reasonable and sifting always brings rewards. The shop specialises in mainstream rock and pop, but there is also a good stock of reggae, country, blues, jazz and classical. When Pete set it up in 1977 with 700 of his own LPs, his customers were mostly punks – 'kids coming in and causing mayhem' – but today the shop is virtually child-free.

The kids have gone digital which, he admits, means nothing to him. Indeed, the digital revolution has had a huge impact on record shops, with a big decline in numbers following the introduction of downloads and streaming. But over the last few years there has been a dramatic recovery, and Sifters has weathered the storm with relative calm.

Admittedly no money is wasted on décor: the walls are papered in faded record posters, the ceiling has rows of vintage strip lights, and the floor is laid with well-worn carpet tiles and furnished with cardboard boxes. But if you are on the lookout for *Highway to Hell*, *London Calling* or *Born to Run*, you could be lucky.

Address 117 Fog Lane, Didsbury, Manchester M20 6FJ, +44 (0)161 445 8697, www.sifters-records-manchester.co.uk | **Getting there** Train to Burnage and 6-minute walk | **Hours** Mon–Tue, Thu–Sat 1–5.30pm | **Tip** Close to Burnage station on Kingsway is the church of St Nicholas by Cachemaille-Day and Lander, a jazzy, streamlined design and one of the most remarkable churches of its date (1932) in Britain.

94 Southern Cemetery Gates
The gates that inspired Morrissey

The Victorian Gothic gates of the largest municipal cemetery in the country are an imposing landmark in south Manchester, although the burial ground itself is one of the least romantic in existence – the land is completely flat and the gravestones are arranged in regular lines stretching as far as the eye can see. The cemetery opened in 1879. Over a century later, the young Morrissey, future frontman of The Smiths, used to spend hours wandering moodily among the memorials, sometimes with his friend Linda Sterling, a performer at the Haçienda and an artist: she designed the famously provocative photomontage for the Buzzcocks 'Orgasm Addict' record sleeve. These walks inspired 'Cemetry Gates' (Morrissey was never very good at spelling), a track from one of The Smiths' greatest albums *The Queen is Dead*, issued in 1986. With music by fellow-Mancunian Johnny Marr and lyrics by Morrissey, the song describes meeting a friend at the gates. They go inside and read the names on the gravestones, they think about the lives of the people buried there, and this leads on to talk about writing, plagiarism and sincerity. The cemetery is a place where Morrissey feels happy and wanted.

Southern Cemetery is the burial place of many famous Mancunians and some infamous ones. They include John and Enriqueta Rylands, of library fame; Sir Matt Busby, legendary manager of Manchester United; the pioneer of transatlantic aviation Sir John Alcock; the painter L. S. Lowry; and Sir Ernest Marples, who brought Premium Bonds, postcodes and motorways to Britain but did a moonlight flit to Monaco to avoid prosecution for tax fraud. Also buried here is the pop impresario Tony Wilson. His unusual gravestone, a slab of shiny black granite with crisp white lettering, was designed by Peter Saville, co-founder with Wilson of Factory Records, and Ben Kelly, designer of the Haçienda.

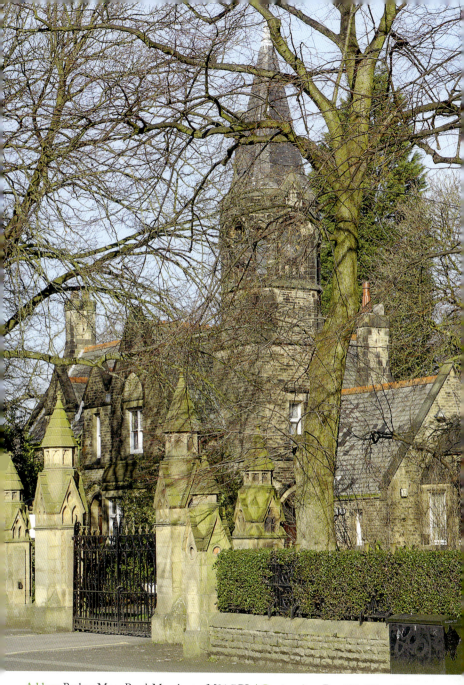

Address Barlow Moor Road, Manchester M21 7GL | **Getting there** Bus 101, 102 or 103 to Southern Cemetery and 5-minute walk | **Hours** Cemetery: daily 8am–dusk | **Tip** On the wall of the disused public lavatories at the junction of Princess Road and Barlow Moor Road is a mural of Alan Turing, the wartime codebreaker and computer genius.

95 The Spärrows
Cross-border comfort food

Here's an original foodie idea: a restaurant serving spätzle, a tender and delicious type of pasta popular across southern Germany, Switzerland, Austria, Hungary, South Tyrol and Trentino-Alto Adige (not to speak of Alsace). Spätzle is a Swabian dialect word meaning sparrows. 'When you traditionally scrub bits of the wet dough into the hot water, they spread out and look like flying birds,' explains Kasia Hitchcock, the Polish co-owner of The Spärrows with her partner, chef Franco Concli, who hails from Trentino in Northern Italy. That explains the name, but their restaurant represents a wider culinary heritage of stuffed pastas and dumplings: gnocchi and ravioli from Italy, pelmeni from Russia, made with thin dough, and the more substantial pierogi from Poland. Spätzle is traditionally served with Käse, a rich sauce made of Emmental and braised onion, but you can mix and match your choice of pasta with various sauces, including a simple butter and sage.

There are also hearty dishes such as Tyrolese beef goulash (milder than the Hungarian variety), smoked sausage with sauerkraut, Swiss fondue and boards of cheeses and cold meats. Matching the cross-continental cuisine is an eclectic choice of drinks, including Swiss beer; wines and spirits from Austria, Hungary, Germany and Italy; and Japanese sake (Kasia is a sake expert, and she has opened Suzume, a sake store and bar, nearby). If you've still not had enough spätzle, you can have them for dessert with cinnamon and brown sugar.

Kasia and Franco first opened The Spärrows in a railway arch in Mirabel Street, a pocket-handkerchief sized restaurant near the Manchester Arena. It was an instant success, and soon they migrated to new premises, also in a railway arch in the up-and-coming Green Quarter. Although larger than their first place, it has the same pleasingly intimate atmosphere and the same modest prices.

Address 16 Red Bank, Green Quarter, Manchester M4 4HF, +44 (0)161 302 6267, www.thesparrows.me, info@thesparrows.me | Getting there Tram (most lines) or train to Victoria and 10-minute walk | Hours Check website for seasonal hours, booking essential | Tip Right behind The Spärrows is the bakery Half Dozen Other, open three mornings a week (Fri 8am, Sat & Sun 9am until sold out). Their breads and cakes are served at Angel Gardens Café, 1 Rochdale Road, a short walk away, and in the city centre at Pot Kettle Black in Barton Arcade (see ch. 12).

96_ Sperm Whale Skeleton
300 dollars' worth of bones

The Living Worlds gallery in the Manchester Museum and the Nature's Library gallery above it contain an incredible array of specimens: birds, bones, beetles, butterflies, minerals, molluscs and mounted animals, such as the majestic Royal Bengal Tiger. Presiding over them all in the central space is the skeleton of a juvenile sperm whale 11 metres long (adults can grow to over 18 metres). The whale was washed up on the coast of Massachusetts in 1896, and the following year the Director of the Manchester Museum bought it for $300. Packed in three crates, it crossed the Atlantic and sailed up the Manchester Ship Canal to Manchester docks. The taxidermist Harry Brazenor took three weeks to put the skeleton back together.

If gigantic skeletons are your thing, there are two more you should see. In the entrance hall is Maharajah, an Asian elephant purchased from a travelling circus in Edinburgh in 1872 by Manchester's now defunct Belle Vue Zoo. Maharajah didn't want to travel by train and smashed up the roof of his special carriage. There was nothing for it but to walk the 200-mile, ten-day journey to Manchester with his keeper. The third skeleton is in the Dinosaurs and Fossils Gallery. You will gasp at Stan, the Tyrannosaurus Rex, but he is a modern cast, taken from a fossilized dinosaur, probably about 66 million years old, discovered in South Dakota in 1987. The original fossil was sold for a record $31.8 million and is now in Abu Dhabi.

These are just three of some 4.5 million items in the Manchester Museum, part of the University of Manchester since 1867. Housed in a Gothic Revival building by the architect Alfred Waterhouse, the museum has undergone a series of refurbishments, including a redisplay of the famous Egyptian mummies and, most recently, new galleries devoted to Chinese and South Asian culture, with a special emphasis on the UK diaspora experience.

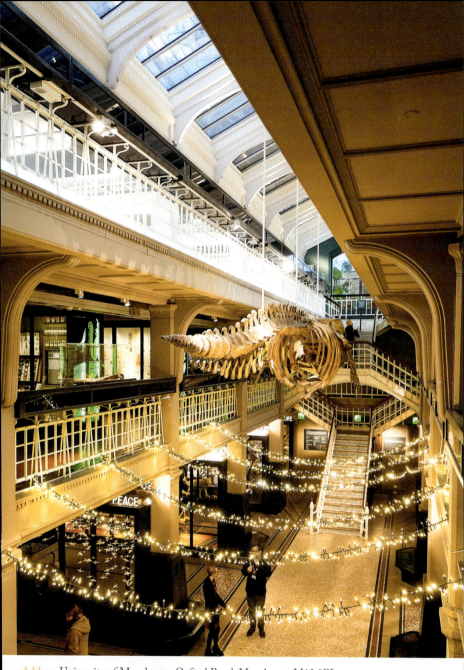

Address University of Manchester, Oxford Road, Manchester M13 9PL www.museum.manchester.ac.uk | **Getting there** Bus 41, 42, 43, 142, 143 | **Hours** Tue, Thu, Fri & Sun 10am–5pm, Wed 10am–9pm, Sat 8am–5pm | **Tip** Behind the Museum extension in Coupland Street is a Blue Plaque on the Rutherford Building, originally called the Physics Laboratory, where Ernest Rutherford discovered the atomic nucleus in 1911 and split the atom in 1919.

97 St George's, Stockport
And glory shone around

Completed in 1898, St George's is one of the largest of all Victorian churches. It has the tallest spire in the Manchester area, and its grandeur recaptures the spirit of the late medieval town churches that inspired its design. The founders were a breakaway group from Stockport's parish church who opposed the rector's high church Anglicanism. One gave the land for a new church, while another, George Fearn, a wealthy brewer, donated the enormous sum of £80,000 to build it. Fearn was a modest man, who kept his patronage secret, but he insisted on a church that would seat at least 1,200 people, substantially more than the bishop thought necessary. For the architect, Herbert Austin of the Lancaster practice Austin and Paley, the commission was a rare gift, and the church was to be his masterpiece.

Seen from Buxton Road, the bulk of the church rears up like a great cliff, with massive buttresses and sheer walls of red sandstone rising to support the heavy crossing tower. Corner pinnacles with flying buttresses steady the lofty spire like the cradle of a skyrocket. The spacious interior is equally dramatic, for immediately on entering, your eye is drawn to the east window, framed by the high tower arches. Both the east and west windows have superb stained glass by Shrigley and Hunt, while virtually all other windows are clear-glazed so that the light pours in, recalling the spirit of East Anglia's great medieval wool churches. The nave roof is timber, with delicate carving that is almost invisible to the eye, while above the sanctuary is a stone vault with foliage and dragons in the bosses. The elaborate reredos is of precious alabaster, and the choir stalls are notable for their large poppy head finials with figures of kings and prophets. Fortunately, this glorious church is beautifully cared for today by a dedicated community who extend a warm welcome to all who visit.

Address 28 Buxton Road, Stockport SK2 6NU, +44 (0)161 480 2453, www.stgeorgestockport.org.uk | Getting there Train to Stockport, then bus 192 from Wellington Road South/Grand Central to St George's Church (direction Hazel Grove) | Hours Wed & Sun 11am – noon | Tip George Fearn's memorial, a scaled-down replica of the church spire, is in the cemetery on the other side of Buxton Road. Turn right at the entrance, second left and the memorial is on the right.

98 Staircase House
A historic house you can touch

Stockport's earliest townhouse dates from the 1460s, when it was a simple cruck-framed dwelling in the market place with a garden stretching down to the river. It was enlarged and remodelled over succeeding centuries, finally falling into ruin before being saved for public view. Its complex history is explained in the audio guide you pick up at the entrance, while the house, free of signage, is what you look at and are encouraged to touch.

The self-guided tour begins at basement level where you pass through dimly lit storerooms roofed with huge rough beams and paved in stone flags. As you progress, the layout of the house and its gradual evolution begin to make sense. In the 16th century, a gabled first floor was added above the original cruck-framed building, and a pair of timber-framed wings and another one in stone were added around an enclosed courtyard. Then in 1605 the building was acquired as a dower house for Mary Shallcross, a member of a wealthy local family, and extensive works were carried out to bring it up to date. These included the insertion of the elaborate cage-newel staircase, after which the house takes its name, and the timber panelling of the front rooms.

The Shallcross family lived here until the 1730s, after which decline set in, with the house being subdivided and let out to grocers, candlemakers and other tradesmen. In 1995 there was a serious fire, the second of two arson attacks, which led to a campaign to save the building. To their credit the council stepped in and bought it, lottery money was secured and architects Donald Insall Associates carried out an exemplary restoration.

Among the delights is a big timber-framed wall, stripped to reveal a patchwork of infill materials: wattle and daub, lath and plaster, bricks, roughcast and clay tiles. Jerry building, or just the natural way that old buildings change?

Address 30–31 Market Place, Stockport SK1 1ES, +44 (0)161 474 4444, www.stockport.gov.uk/topic/staircase-house | **Getting there** Train to Stockport and 10-minute walk via St Petersgate | **Hours** Wed & Thu 10am–5pm, Fri noon–5pm, Sat 10am–5pm, Sun 11am–4pm | **Tip** At nearby 23-25 Little Underbank is a splendid clock with figures including Father Time with his scythe that used to surmount a jewellers' shop. Recently restored, it chimes the quarter hour once again.

99 Stockport Air Raid Shelters
The Chestergate Hotel

During the wartime Blitz, thousands of Stockport's citizens sought refuge in a labyrinth of tunnels carved out of solid rock. The tunnels were created in 1938 when underground cellars were discovered below a group of properties on Chestergate and it was decided to extend them as air-raid shelters. Closed up and long forgotten after war ended, this underground world tells a moving story of Britain under bombardment.

On entering the tunnels, you will see the marks of the pneumatic drills used to cut through the stone. It took over a year of digging, a two-man team progressing a mere one metre a day, but when finished the tunnels were big enough for 6,500 people. You can hear radio announcements from the BBC offering advice on public health – anyone you see spitting must be reported. There are also instructions on how to make the most of children's clothes – 'Father's old flannel trousers are useful for making a warm little frock,' – while the Ministry of Food enthusiastically promotes the benefits of eating dried egg.

The Blitz hit London in September 1940 and on 22 December almost 300 German aircraft attacked Manchester for 12 hours, dropping high-explosive bombs and incendiary devices. Over this and the next day, 30,000 houses were damaged and 5,000 people were made homeless. In the shelters, there was fear and discomfort, but there was also camaraderie. The women from the WRVS made endless cups of tea, and street entertainers played wartime favourites on squeezeboxes and mouth organs. There was electric lighting, bench seating, flush and chemical toilets, a pair of wardens and a first-aid post staffed by nurses from the local hospital. A place of safety from the devastation, the Stockport shelters soon gained the nickname of The Chestergate Hotel.

Address 65 Great Underbank, Stockport SK1 1NE, +44 (0)161 474 1940, www.stockport.gov.uk/topic/air-raid-shelters | Getting there Train to Stockport and 10-minute walk via Chestergate | Hours Tue–Fri 1–5pm, Sat 10am–5pm, Sun 11am–4pm | Tip Stockport Art Gallery on Wellington Road South doubles as an impressive War Memorial.

100_ The Temple
From water closet to watering place

Beneath a traffic island in Great Bridgewater Street is one of the smallest and oddest bars in Manchester. Its name comes from Lucinda Lambton's book *Temples of Convenience*, which celebrates the splendours of the Victorian lavatory; for this is what The Temple used to be.

With a set of steps leading down at each end, it consists of a narrow space with banquettes along the walls and 10 tiny tables packed together to create a very sociable atmosphere. Little effort has been wasted on interior decoration, the green and cream-tiled walls have been well scrubbed, and the concrete floor and ceiling coated in a thick layer of black gloss paint. Drinks, mostly bottled beers with some on tap, a good range of whiskies and well-priced bottles of wine, are dispensed from a small counter at one end. At the other end is a pair of toilet cubicles with a display of unprintable graffiti noted for its alcohol-inspired Manchester wit.

The Temple's treasure is the jukebox, which offers a selection of Manchester sounds and earlier classics. The pub is a favourite haunt of indie band Elbow's vocalist Guy Garvey, who immortalised it in the band's song 'Grounds for Divorce' where he describes it as a hole in his neighbourhood that he couldn't help falling into.

Public lavatories were once commonplace in Manchester, fulfilling a need now catered for by the ubiquitous coffee bar. There were smart underground ladies' and gents' facilities in the centre of Albert Square, and rows of sordid urinals behind a hole in the wall under Deansgate Station and in a brick kiosk below the railway viaduct on Oxford Street. All have disappeared in the interests of health and safety, with not a thought given to their potential reuse. Don't miss out on the chance of enjoying a pint, spending a penny and having a chat with a friendly drinking crowd in a former Temple of Convenience.

Address 100 Great Bridgewater Street, Manchester M1 5JW, +44 (0)161 278 1610 | **Getting there** Tram to St Peter's Square (all lines) | **Hours** Mon–Thu 3pm–midnight, Fri & Sat 3pm–1am, Sun 3.30pm–midnight | **Tip** Manchester's oldest *pissotière*, last used in 1896, was at 36 Charles Street as recorded in a plaque on the wall of the Lass O'Gowrie pub.

101_ Tower of Light
The world's most beautiful flue

The strange white tower piercing the skyline in the heart of the city harks back to Manchester's history as the first industrial city. For when the Council announced its intention to be carbon zero by 2038, they decided to lead the way and to do it in style.

The Tower of Light may be just a flue, but in its design and engineering it recaptures the spirit of innovation and technical skill that made the city great 200 years ago. The landmark Tower and the Wall of Energy to which it is attached are the visible parts of a mostly underground low-carbon energy centre providing heat and power to the city's network of major civic buildings including the Town Hall, Central Library, City Art Gallery and Bridgewater Hall.

Designed by architects Tonkin Liu, the Tower follows a construction method called 'shell lace structure', inspired by the geometry of the natural world to minimise the amount of material used. The super-thin steel skin, stiffened by undulations like those of a seashell, is a lightweight lattice that is more perforated towards the top where less strength is required. The adjoining Wall of Energy is faced in glazed ceramic tiles that reflect light and movement of the clouds, their interlocking pattern reminiscent of marks left in the sand by ocean waves. Within a structure inspired by nature, the workings of the energy centre can be viewed through a long ribbon window. By day, sunlight bounces off reflectors set inside the Tower, while at night it is illuminated with a shifting programme of colours to suit the occasion. Car lights that flicker across the rippling tiles add to the animation. With the principal materials – steel and ceramics – both made by Lancashire companies, Shawston Engineering and Darwen Terracotta, plus the beauty of the structure, this new landmark is a strong statement of the Council's commitment to innovation and clean energy.

Address 50 Great Bridgewater Street, Manchester, M1 5LE | **Getting there** Tram to St Peter's Square (all lines) | **Hours** Accessible 24 hours | **Tip** Manchester is becoming a city of towers, with skyscrapers popping up everywhere. The tallest and largest group is the nearby Deansgate Square, completed in 2022.

102 — Twenty Twenty Two
Bats in the basement

Bored with your usual watering-hole? Looking for something a bit different? Try this one: it's a ping-pong bar. Not a table tennis bar. Table tennis is the professional championship game, where players deploy the different textures of rubber bats to generate speed and spin. What you play here is ping-pong, the recreational version, using sandpaper bats. Anyone can have a go, and it's only 12 quid for an hour: you don't even have to buy a drink, although why wouldn't you? Whether you are a spectator or a player, the back room of Twenty Twenty Two, with its line of six tables, is a lot of fun. There is something mesmeric about watching people play, especially if you have a drink in your hand, your eyes swivelling from one side to the other as the balls bounce back and forth.

While ping-pong is the main event at Twenty Twenty Two, it's not the whole experience. You come here for ping-pong, you get industrial archaeology with authentic Manchester grittiness thrown in – exposed concrete floors, cast-iron columns, and once-white tiles, now chipped and cracked with age. It's a utilitarian space that used to be the basement of a textile warehouse: this is where the cloth was weighed, compacted using hydraulic presses, and packed, before being despatched across the Empire. Above the ledges where you sit to watch the games, the windows have been angled to admit maximum daylight from the sooty atmosphere outside. The place is given a modern spin with a giant screen showing trashy American movies, while on the walls is a backdrop of colourful murals and tags, regularly refreshed by local street artists, so that the place looks different every time you go.

Darts, pool and other games are also on offer and at weekends, it can get crowded as there's a DJ keeping the space throbbing until late, with bouncers and queues outside. Better to go on a Thursday for Beat the Bartender – if you win the game, you get a free round.

Address Twenty Twenty Two, The Basement, Little Lever Street, Manchester M1 1EZ, +44 (0)161 237 9368, www.twentytwentytwo.co.uk | Getting there 4–minute walk from Piccadilly Gardens | **Hours** Sun–Tue 3pm–1am, Fri 3pm–3am, Sat 1pm–3am | Tip Fans of film, trashy or otherwise, will love Mini Cini, a 36-seat cinema showing classic and alternative film. It's part of the Ducie Street Warehouse, a stylish ex-industrial conversion with a hotel, restaurant, bar and event spaces (www.duciestreet.com).

103 — Unicorn Grocery
Did you bring your own bag?

What's a supermarket doing in a book like this? You wouldn't call Unicorn Grocery quirky, but it certainly is different, even though this medium-sized supermarket sells many of the same things you will find in Sainsbury's or Tesco. Unicorn is an independent in an age dominated by corporates; it is democratically run as a workers' co-operative with a flat management structure and equal pay; and its range of food, drink and household items emphasises local, organic and fairtrade, with no animal products, genetically modified ingredients or foods full of chemical additives and excessive amounts of sugar and salt.

From small beginnings in 1996 Unicorn has become one of Britain's largest independent wholefood groceries with an annual turnover of around £7 million and a range of over 2,500 product lines. How have they done it? Unicorn avoids middlemen, buying direct from manufacturers or growers where possible, and often in bulk. Over 90 per cent of their British fruit and vegetables come straight from the farm gate, mostly local. Packaging is kept to a minimum and carried out on site, saving money. A lot of produce is sold unwrapped, with customers encouraged to bring their own containers and bags. Why aren't all supermarkets like this?

The greengrocery shelves are vibrant with colour and aroma; there's a children's play area; and who can resist the delicatessen counter, with salads, curries and soups freshly made in the kitchen upstairs? Artisan breads come from a co-op in Yorkshire and a family bakery in Derbyshire, and samosas from Ashton-under-Lyne. In case you are thinking this is an expensive enclave for south Manchester's *Guardian*-toting right-on brigade seeking ingredients for the latest Ottolenghi, you will be surprised at who comes here and even more amazed at Unicorn's price comparison board – most of their stuff really is cheaper than the big boys.

Address 89 Albany Road, Chorlton, Manchester M21 0BN, +44 (0)161 861 0010, www.unicorn-grocery.coop | **Getting there** Tram to Chorlton (pink, grey or navy lines) and 5-minute walk; or bus 86 to Kensington Road | **Hours** Tue–Fri 9.30am–7pm, Sat 9am–6pm, Sun 11am–5pm | **Tip** Quentin Crisp, author of *The Naked Civil Servant*, died in Chorlton while touring his one-man show. There is a Banksy-style mural of him by street-artist Stewy on Keppel Road near the corner with Wilbraham Road (4-minute walk).

104 — Valette's Albert Square
Still in the heart of Manchester

The French artist Adolphe Valette came to Manchester in 1905 to study at the School of Art and was soon promoted to the post of Art Master (L. S. Lowry was one of his pupils). Steeped in Impressionism, Valette depicted workaday Manchester as an atmospheric city of shifting mists, with the outlines of buildings blurred by the damp, soot-laden air; people simplified into silhouettes; and with the new motor cars and trams appearing alongside the picturesque horse-drawn cabs that were soon to vanish from the cobbled streets.

The main structures he depicted in his view of Albert Square, painted in 1910, are still very much with us today, apart from the power lines of the electric tram system seen at the top. On the left is the Albert Memorial, by Manchester architect Thomas Worthington, still at the centre of the square. Prince Albert died in 1861 and the Manchester monument, built soon afterwards, was the first to the Prince Consort to place the statue under a Gothic canopy; it was designed shortly before the more famous Albert Memorial in London. The white marble statue just beyond the memorial represents John Bright, the Rochdale-born politician and advocate of free trade; it dates from 1901 while the statue with one arm raised is a bronze of 1878, showing the Liberal Prime Minister W. E. Gladstone pointing the way, it used to be said, to Central Station. Lording it over the square on the right is the Town Hall, the Gothic revival masterpiece of the architect Alfred Waterhouse, begun in 1867 and opened a decade later.

Albert Square is still Manchester's principal civic space. One side of the square has been rebuilt, but the Town Hall, no longer soot-blackened, still exemplifies Manchester's civic pride. It is currently closed for major restoration works until 2026, when this municipal palace will once again be open for all to admire and celebrate.

Address Albert Square, Manchester M2 5DB | Getting there Tram to St Peter's Square (all lines) | Tip The Valette painting is normally on display with others by him at Manchester Art Gallery in Mosley Street, a few minutes' walk away from Albert Square.

105 Victoria Baths
A water palace refreshed

Manchester's most prized public baths gained national attention in 2003 when it won the BBC's *Restoration* programme and received a £3.5-million National Lottery grant for much-needed repairs. Some 10 years earlier the baths had been closed down; but such was the opposition that local people formed a trust and took control of maintenance and fundraising to secure its future. The lottery money saved the building from demolition, but the struggle continues as you will hear if you take a tour of the premises with one of the enthusiastic volunteer guides.

When built in 1906, Victoria Baths was a showpiece bathing institution. It included three swimming pools – Males 1st class, Males 2nd class and Females (social status was as important as gender at that time) – Turkish and Russian Baths, 64 wash baths, a laundry and club rooms. The 1st class males (also known as the Gala Pool) and the female baths retain their original changing cubicles around the pool edges, and throughout the building are floor-to-ceiling decorative tiles, mosaic floors and colourful stained-glass windows. The once popular Turkish Baths are a series of tile-clad chambers with under-floor heating and marble benches. Many children learned to swim in the pools, and two world famous swimmers trained here: Sunny Lowry, one of the first women to swim the Channel, and John Besford, who won the 1934 European 100 metres backstroke title in Magdeburg, much to the disgust of Hitler who was rooting for the German champion Ernst Küppers.

Now, more than 30 years after the baths closed, the vision has not been dulled. Having returned the building to sound condition, the next phase is the restoration of the Turkish Baths, and then the reopening of the Gala Pool. There is a welcoming café, a well-stocked shop and an exhibition area. Almost as impressive is the commitment of the trust and its volunteers to the building they love.

Address Hathersage Road, Manchester M13 0FE, +44 (0)161 224 2020, www.victoriabaths.org.uk | **Getting there** Bus 41, 44, 48, 192 to Hathersage Road | **Hours** April–Sept Wed 11am–3pm. Otherwise, visit website for open days and events which extend from March–Nov or phone to check if open on a certain date. | **Tip** Ashton Old Baths is another impressive public baths, although it has been remodelled as shared workspaces. Contact info@ashtonoldbaths.co.uk for details of tours.

106 — Walkden Gardens
A garden of many rooms

Hidden away in the Manchester suburbs is a little-known garden of exceptional quality. It is named after Harry Walkden who lived in the house next door and left the land to Sale Council in 1949. The garden was created by the council's head gardener Louis Bell in the 1950s, and has been greatly enhanced by the energetic Friends of Walkden Gardens in recent years. Bell divided the land, which had previously been a plant nursery, into a series of interlinked garden 'rooms' surrounded by hedges, each with its own distinctive character. These are revealed in turn as you walk around.

The journey begins at the compass point, a paved rotunda with a pebble mosaic giving directions to the various parts of the garden. Among these are the woodland walk, the wisteria arch, the theatre lawn, the birch walk and the field of hope. There is also a fuchsia garden, a conifer garden and a cherry walk. Most remarkable is the Japanese garden, which was created in 2006 by the Japanese Garden Society. It follows the 'stroll garden' type that affords changing views as the visitor walks through it, and is divided into three parts. The first focuses on a rock formation representing three welcoming Buddhist deities; the second is much larger with more naturalistic planting to represent a woodland grove; and the third is a dry landscape garden with gravel suggesting a lake, rocks as islands and a mountain range. As with the best Japanese gardens it engenders a feeling of calmness and relaxation. Very different is the labyrinth, which opened in 2018 and was inspired by the one at Chartres Cathedral.

Don't miss the historic dovecote, which was originally built in the grounds of nearby Sale Hall, but was saved from destruction caused by the widening of the M60 motorway and moved brick by brick to the gardens where it is used for exhibitions, art workshops and serving ice cream.

Address Derbyshire Road, Sale M33 3EL, www.walkdengardens.co.uk | **Getting there** Tram to Brooklands (purple or green line) and 15-minute walk along Marsland Road | **Hours** Daily, summer 9am–7pm, winter 9am–4.30pm | **Tip** On the opposite side of Marsland Road is the Moorfield pub, formerly a hotel with a strange tower that was built in the 1870s to serve adjoining pleasure gardens that have now given way to housing.

107_ The Wash House
Rinse and spin

There's something funny about that launderette on Shudehill. Maybe it's the ancient packet of Daz that has been standing on the washing machine for months, or maybe it's the people who go in there – none of them ever seems to be carrying any dirty laundry – and did you ever hear of a launderette where you have to book? The only way to solve the mystery is to give it a try. Book; arrive; pick up the retro telephone to announce yourself; open the door of the spin dryer and enter – inside, instead of whiter than white it's darker than dark, there's a buzz of conversation and a groovy house soundtrack accompanied by swishing cocktail shakers. Oh – it's a speakeasy.

Whoever wrote the menu must have done the MA in Creative Writing at Manchester Uni: 'rich, velveteen, tannic and comforting' is the description of Tea-Total, based on rum with tea liqueur, sherry and egg, while This Mary Ain't Going No-where, a twist on a classic Bloody Mary, is 'savoury, filling, spicy and meaty' (it's made with Bury Black Pudding). Or maybe the mixologist took his degree in Local History, as cocktails are dedicated to Manchester themes including vermouth-based Suffragette City ('fragrant, sharp, alluring, deceptive') and Turing's Daisy, made with gin, bergamot and lemongrass (it comes with a padlock that has to be decoded). What would the city fathers think of downing a Concilio et Labore ('light, floral, honeyed, herbaceous') and how would Engels rate The Condition of the Working Class ('cheesy and involving')?

The bartenders are friendly, the snacks are moreish and the cocktails have eye-appeal – Botanical Garden comes in a miniature glasshouse arranged with fresh flowers, and a mini-slice of Battenberg adorns Let Them Eat Cake. For the connoisseur, the array of recherché ingredients and flavour combinations is impressive; for the novice, just sink into the leather sofas and let it all wash over you.

Address 19 Shudehill, Manchester M4 2AF, www.washhousemcr.com | **Getting there** Tram (most lines) or bus to Shudehill | **Hours** Mon–Thu 4pm–1am, Fri & Sat noon–2am, Sun 3–11pm | **Tip** A few doors up Shudehill is Paramount Books, stuffed with second-hand books of all kinds but specialising in vintage comics and magazines (open Sat & Sun noon–late).

108   Where the Light Gets In
Not so much a meal as an experience

Sam Buckley's quirky Stockport restaurant is a barn-like space on the top floor of an old coffee warehouse with rough brick walls and large windows; dried corn cobs hanging from the roof beams and Ercol dining tables and chairs impart a rustic feel. A huge open kitchen occupies half the room, with half-a-dozen chefs working in a calm, unhurried way right under the diners' noses.

There are no menus: dishes are devised daily using meat and fish from trusted small producers, and vegetables and herbs foraged in the wild or grown on Sam's kitchen garden, which believe it or not is on the roof of Stockport's Merseyway Shopping Centre. Home-made pickles and ferments add depth and complexity. Understanding what you are eating is part of the fun: a succession of small plates is brought to your table by informally dressed servers alternating with the chefs themselves, and all are happy to explain and discuss. Ingredients, whether homely or unusual (bull's testicles and monkfish livers have figured), are presented on varying styles of crockery from rough earthenware to fragile porcelain. Carlingford oysters with apple oil and whey are preceded by oyster shells filled with oyster dip and amazing brassica crisps. Tender potato morsels with green garlic oil come in a velvety soup made of three potato varieties. A small Staffordshire farm supplies free-range chicken ('it led a happy life'), a disc of breast meat wrapped in cabbage accompanied by a sliver of chicken thigh. A cigarette of chopped beetroot sits next to a glossy mound of green watercress sauce. For dessert, rhubarb ripple ice cream or Bakewell tart with a twist. There are tasty sourdough breads, home-made chutneys on the cheese plate, and pairings with recherché wines and fresh or fermented juices. Expensive – yes – but wholly memorable. Slow down and savour: even tasting-menu-sceptics will be won over.

Address 7 Rostron Brow, Stockport SK1 1JY, +44 (0)161 477 5744, www.wtlgi.co | Getting there Train to Stockport and 10-minute walk | Hours Booking in advance essential, see website for dates and times | Tip Just round the corner at 15 Lower Hillgate Sam Buckley has opened Yellowhammer, a sourdough bakery, pottery studio and (evenings Thu–Sat) a restaurant (check www.yellowhammer-stockport.co.uk for hours).

109 Whitworth Garden
Art in the park

Ever since it was built, the Whitworth Art Gallery turned its back on Whitworth Park, but the £15 million extension that opened in 2015 has reversed this, bringing art and nature together. The Art Garden, enclosed by two new glass wings, was designed by Sarah Price, who created the 2012 Olympic meadows. Her Whitworth planting of perennials and grasses is edged by clouds of evergreen box, forming abstract patterns across the landscape. The garden's character changes through the seasons, first with colourful spring bulbs and later with towering summer perennials. Further out, the planting becomes sparser and merges into newly established grassland, strengthening the link between gallery, garden and park. Also by Price is the Alex Bernstein Garden, a secluded space planted with wildflowers to attract insects, butterflies and bees (there are hives on the gallery roof). To see this garden, you have to enter the gallery and go out again through a glass door just past the lift.

The park's trees and planting provide the backdrop for outdoor sculpture. Just beyond the Art Garden in the trees is *Bending Figure* by Raqs Media Collective of New Delhi. It includes quotes from Orwell's *Shooting an Elephant* and refers to the neglected Imperial statuary of British India, evoking the hubris of pomp and circumstance. The Bernstein Garden houses Emily Young's *Maremma Warrior Head V*, made from a block of ancient quartzite, and reminds us of the passing of time. A different material is used for *The Obelisk* at the centre of the park, created by Cyprien Gaillard. This was made out of crushed brick and concrete from demolished housing in nearby Hulme and Moss Side. Further on is *Flailing Trees* – 21 upended willow trees embedded in concrete – a protest by Gustav Metzger at human aggression against nature. It is good to see that both art gallery and park have benefited from the recent renaissance.

Address Whitworth Art Gallery, Oxford Road, Manchester M14 4PW, +44 (0)161 275 7450, www.whitworth.manchester.ac.uk | **Getting there** Bus 41, 42, 43 and 143 from city centre to Whitworth Park | **Hours** Park daily dawn–dark, gallery Tue & Wed 10am–5pm, Thu 10am–9pm, Fri–Sun 10am–5pm | **Tip** The Whitworth Gallery café, serving breakfast through to evening meals during gallery opening hours, provides beautiful views over the park and Art Garden.

110_ Worsley Delph
Coals to Manchester

A transport revolution began in Worsley when Francis Egerton, 3rd Duke of Bridgewater, built a canal to transport coal from the mines on his estate direct to Manchester. The most daring feature of the Bridgewater Canal was the underground waterways driven into the rockface from the canal basin at Worsley Delph to connect with the mines. Over time, 46 miles of tunnels were constructed, on four different levels, connected by a water-powered railway incline and lifts. The incline had a lock at the upper level where the boat would enter and be seated on a wagon. When the water was drained, it would be lowered on ropes, descending 32 metres, counterbalanced by a second boat ascending a parallel railway track. In this way, the coal could be lifted to the main level and go on to Manchester without changing boats.

Overgrown and hidden for many years, the Delph (an old English word for a quarry) can now be clearly seen from a new multilevel viewing gallery. The water-filled Delph is contained on the north side by a cliff face in which two tunnel entrances are visible. Between the tunnels is a quayside with a tall rotating structure, a contemporary interpretation of a curious crane that is known from descriptions to have been used to lift stones from the quarry into barges. Other evocative objects placed on the viewing gallery include miners' hats, a pickaxe and shovel, and a coal cart with harness that was commonly towed by women, all cast in bronze. Statements by children as young as seven give a picture of what it was like in the mines before child labour was outlawed in 1842; one, whose job it was to stand all day opening and closing a door, never saw daylight except on Sundays. The construction of the canal halved the price of coal in Manchester, and made a fortune for the Egerton family, but at what cost to the Worsley miners and their families?

Address School Brow, Worsley M28 2GD | **Getting there** Bus 33 to Worsley Court House | **Hours** Accessible 24 hours | **Tip** After the underground canals closed in 1887, Worsley was remodelled as a picturesque village. One of many early features to remain is the Alphabet Bridge over the canal, so christened by local schoolchildren who used its 26 planks to practise their alphabets.

111_Yes
Positive thinking on four floors

With two food outlets and an outdoor roof terrace, as well as two live music spaces, Yes changes its personality across the day, offering a different experience on each of its four floors. Formerly an auction room, and before that a printing works, the building has a gritty industrial character with heavy steel beams, chunky metal staircase and exposed plumbing. Downstairs is a dark basement club that houses free disco sessions, and on the first floor is the Pink Room, a larger gig venue decked out in shocking pink. On the ground floor is the main bar with a good selection of beers including Lagunitas IPA and Ancoats-brewed ShinDigger Mango Unchained, sold at competitive prices. Place your order for tasty street food from the open kitchen offering made-to-order pizza slices by Pepperoni Playboy – and you're given a cunning device that pings to tell you when your dish is ready to collect.

Catch the evening sun in the attic bar, opening onto a high terrace, cleverly formed by partially removing the roof. You can sit outside overlooking the tower of the Kimpton (see ch. 59) and watch the trains rattling by on the viaduct connecting Oxford Road and Piccadilly Stations. Here cocktails include Tonka and Pearl, Hacienda G&T, New York Cherry or maybe try a Toffee and Amaro. Both bars open at noon equipped with fast track wifi and comfortable seating where you can spend time with friends.

The hip music promoters Now Wave, who created the venue in 2018, feature favoured solo artists such as Cornish singer Gwenno and Indie rock band Boy Azooga, together with more esoteric sounds. The repertoire includes jazz and soul as well as post-punk, rap and alternative rock and roll, with ace acoustics in the Pink Room. Don't miss the Andy Warhol lookalike film on the staircase. It's mesmerising. With all this going on, you can happily spend a day eating, drinking, socialising and grooving to the music at Yes.

Address 38 Charles Street, Manchester M1 7DB, +44 (0)161 273 2725, www.yes-manchester.com | **Getting there** Train to Oxford Road Station and 4–minute walk | **Hours** Daily noon–late | **Tip** Visit the site of Rafters, legendary music venue from the punk era at 65 Oxford Street, a former theatre within the St James' Building (it is now Tesco Metro). The career of Joy Division was launched here, and The Smiths, Depeche Mode and Generation X also performed.

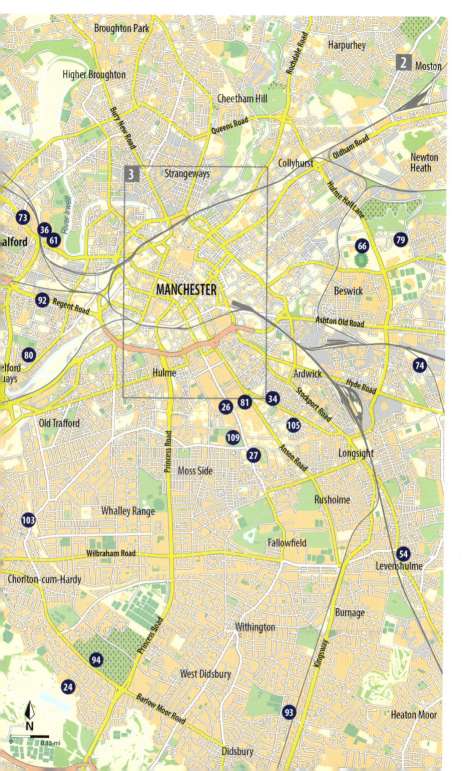

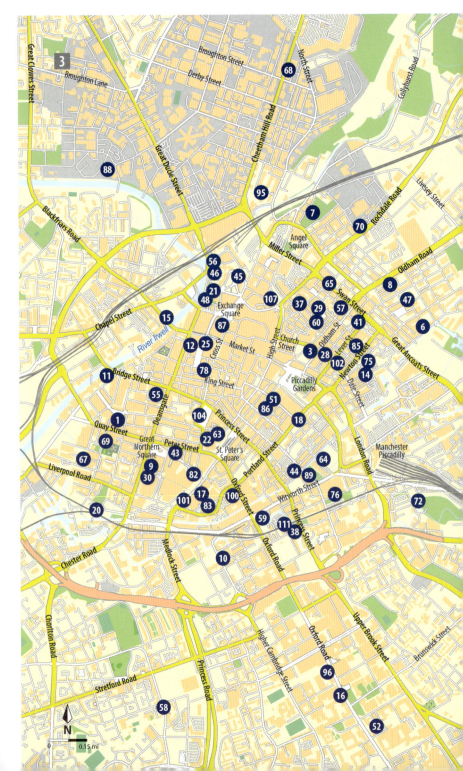

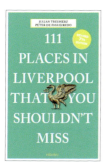

Julian Treuherz,
Peter de Figueiredo
**111 Places in Liverpool
That You Shouldn't Miss**
ISBN 978-3-7408-2515-7

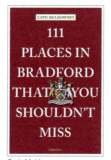

Cath Muldowney
**111 Places in Bradford
That You Shouldn't Miss**
ISBN 978-3-7408-1427-4

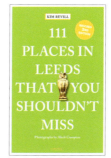

Kim Revill, Alesh Compton
**111 Places in Leeds
That You Shouldn't Miss**
ISBN 978-3-7408-2059-6

Michael Glover, Richard Anderson
**111 Places in Sheffield
That You Shouldn't Miss**
ISBN 978-3-7408-2348-1

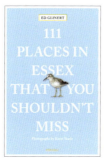

Ed Glinert, Karin Tearle
**111 Places in Essex
That You Shouldn't Miss**
ISBN 978-3-7408-1593-6

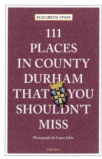

Elizabeth Atkin, Laura Atkin
**111 Places in County Durham
That You Shouldn't Miss**
ISBN 978-3-7408-1426-7

David Taylor
**111 Places along Hadrian's Wall
That You Shouldn't Miss**
ISBN 978-3-7408-1425-0

Ed Glinert, David Taylor
**111 Places in Yorkshire
That You Shouldn't Miss**
ISBN 978-3-7408-1167-9

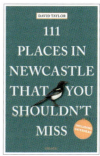

David Taylor
**111 Places in Newcastle
That You Shouldn't Miss**
ISBN 978-3-7408-1043-6

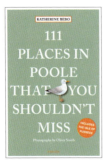

Katherine Bebo, Oliver Smith
**111 Places in Poole
That You Shouldn't Miss**
ISBN 978-3-7408-0598-2

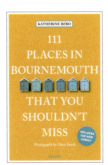

Katherine Bebo, Oliver Smith
**111 Places in Bournemouth
That You Shouldn't Miss**
ISBN 978-3-7408-2646-8

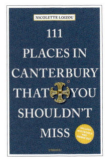

Nicolette Loizou
**111 Places in Canterbury
That You Shouldn't Miss**
ISBN 978-3-7408-0899-0

Philip R. Stone
**111 Dark Places in England
That You Shouldn't Miss**
ISBN 978-3-7408-0900-3

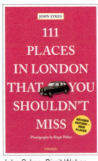

John Sykes, Birgit Weber
**111 Places in London
That You Shouldn't Miss**
ISBN 978-3-7408-1644-5

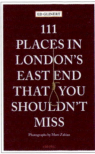

Ed Glinert, Marc Zakian
**111 Places in London's East End
That You Shouldn't Miss**
ISBN 978-3-7408-0752-8

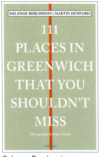

Solange Berchemin,
Martin Dunford, Karin Tearle
**111 Places in Greenwich
That You Shouldn't Miss**
ISBN 978-3-7408-1107-5

Nicola Perry, Daniel Reiter
**33 Walks in London
That You Shouldn't Miss**
ISBN 978-3-7408-1955-2

Kirstin von Glasow
**111 Gardens in London
That You Shouldn't Miss**
ISBN 978-3-7408-0143-4

Laura Richards, Jamie Newson
**111 London Pubs and Bars
That You Shouldn't Miss**
ISBN 978-3-7408-0893-8

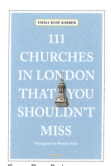

Emma Rose Barber,
Benedict Flett
**111 Churches in London
That You Shouldn't Miss**
ISBN 978-3-7408-0901-0

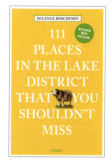

Solange Berchemin
**111 Places in the Lake District
That You Shouldn't Miss**
ISBN 978-3-7408-2404-4

Rob Ganley, Ian Williams
**111 Places in Coventry
That You Shouldn't Miss**
ISBN 978-3-7408-1044-3

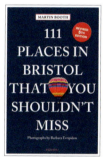

Martin Booth, Barbara Evripidou
**111 Places in Bristol
That You Shouldn't Miss**
ISBN 978-3-7408-2512-6

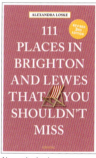

Alexandra Loske
**111 Places in Brighton and
Lewes That You Shouldn't Miss**
ISBN 978-3-7408-1727-5

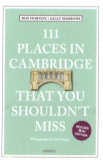

Rosalind Horton, Sally Simmons,
Guy Snape
**111 Places in Cambridge
That You Shouldn't Miss**
ISBN 978-3-7408-2376-4

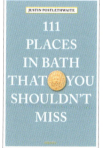

Justin Postlethwaite
**111 Places in Bath
That You Shouldn't Miss**
ISBN 978-3-7408-0146-5

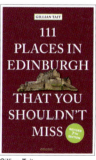

Gillian Tait
**111 Places in Edinburgh
That You Shouldn't Miss**
ISBN 978-3-7408-2575-1

Tom Shields, Gillian Tait
**111 Places in Glasgow
That You Shouldn't Miss**
ISBN 978-3-7408-2237-8

Kai Oidtmann
**111 Places in Iceland
That You Shouldn't Miss**
ISBN 978-3-7408-0030-7

Andrea Livnat,
Angelika Baumgartner
**111 Places in Tel Aviv
That You Shouldn't Miss**
ISBN 978-3-7408-0263-9

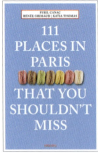

Sybil Canac, Renée Grimaud,
Katia Thomas
**111 Places in Paris
That You Shouldn't Miss**
ISBN 978-3-7408-0159-5

Thomas Fuchs
**111 Places in Amsterdam
That You Shouldn't Miss**
ISBN 978-3-7408-0023-9

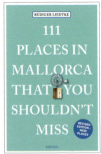

Rüdiger Liedtke
**111 Places in Mallorca
That You Shouldn't Miss**
ISBN 978-3-7408-1049-8

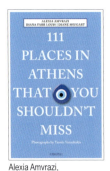

Alexia Amvrazi,
Diana Farr Louis, Diane Shugart,
Yannis Varouhakis
**111 Places in Athens
That You Shouldn't Miss**
ISBN 978-3-7408-0377-3

Christine Izeki, Björn Neumann
**111 Places in Tokyo
That You Shouldn't Miss**
ISBN 978-3-7408-1277-5

Christoph Hein, Sabine Hein
**111 Places in Singapore
That You Shouldn't Miss**
ISBN 978-3-7408-0382-7

Special thanks to: Perry Bonewell; Geoff Brown; Sam Buckley; Jenny and William Cragg; Alexandra Cropper; Philippa Duxbury; David Gelsthorpe; Martin Glynn; Elaine Griffiths; Leslie Holmes; Paula Hope; Ros Horton; Liam Jackson; Nigel Lawson; Lyn McKay; Rebecca Milner; Peter Nears; John Peel; Eddy Rhead; Nita Saleem; Howard Smith; Moira Stevenson; Tim, Richard and Nick Treuherz; Ian and Katie Wray; and the late Gill Wright.

Peter de Figueiredo was brought up in Cheshire, studying architecture at the Manchester School of Art and urban design at the University of Manchester, leading to a career in historic buildings conservation. For many years he was based at the Manchester office of English Heritage, before running his own consultancy.

Julian Treuherz was born in Littleborough and went to school in Manchester, when he first got to know the city. He later returned to work as a curator at the Manchester Art Gallery before disappearing down the M62 to head up the art galleries in another big city nearby. He is an expert on Victorian art and the Pre-Raphaelites.

Peter de Figueiredo and Julian Treuherz are the joint authors of the bestselling *111 Places in Liverpool That You Shouldn't Miss*.

The information in this book was accurate at the time of publication, but it can change at any time. Please confirm the details for the places you're planning to visit before you head out on your adventures.